D1039569

THE SIN OF WHITE SUPREMACY

THE SIN OF WHITE SUPREMACY

Christianity, Racism, and
Religious Diversity in America

JEANNINE HILL FLETCHER

ORBIS BOOKS
Maryknoll, New York 10545

Founded in 1970, Orbis Books endeavors to publish works that enlighten the mind, nourish the spirit, and challenge the conscience. The publishing arm of the Maryknoll Fathers and Brothers, Orbis seeks to explore the global dimensions of the Christian faith and mission, to invite dialogue with diverse cultures and religious traditions, and to serve the cause of reconciliation and peace. The books published reflect the views of their authors and do not represent the official position of the Maryknoll Society. To learn more about Maryknoll and Orbis Books, please visit our website at www.maryknollsociety.org.

Library of Congress Cataloging-in-Publication Data

Names: Hill Fletcher, Jeannine, author.
Title: The sin of white supremacy : Christianity, racism, and religious
  diversity in America / by Jeannine Hill Fletcher.
Description: Maryknoll : Orbis Books, 2017. | Includes bibliographical
  references and index.
Identifiers: LCCN 2017002613 (print) | LCCN 2017022766 (ebook) |
  ISBN 9781608337026 (e-book) | ISBN 9781626982376 (pbk.)
Subjects: LCSH: Racism—United States. | White supremacy movements—
  United States. | Race relations—Religious aspects—Christianity. | Church
  and social problems—United States. | Whites—United States—Race
  identity. | United States—Race relations.
Classification: LCC E184.A1 (ebook) | LCC E184.A1 H528 2017 (print) |
  DDC 305.800973—dc23
LC record available at https://lccn.loc.gov/2017002613

For Sandra, Justin, Kathy, Beta, Kate, and Melissa
and
Owen, Ella, and Thea

CONTENTS

PREFACE

I KNOW A LOT OF "good Christians" and "nice White people" troubled by the disparity they see in our world. They can see the segregation that still structures our neighborhoods, and this disappoints them. They recognize the struggles of urban youth and feel bad that such tragedies as failing schools, gang violence, and drugs still plague our communities. They make service trips to the inner city or reservations to try to help people. The escalation of police brutality toward people of color and the strains on our national psyche fifty years after the height of the civil rights movement genuinely trouble them. It is with sadness that they see our non-Christian neighbors targeted and subjected to suspicion. They wish our world was different.

But most among my good White Christian friends do not see very clearly the way the disparity and injustice we experience today has been legislated by the United States since the beginning of its history. They see these as problems of the inner city, or the Black community, or immigrants, but they do not necessarily see these problems as their own. Many may recognize vaguely that our current conditions are the result of generational dispossession, but few among us have been given the tools to analyze our world critically. Those good White Christians involved in service work to the impoverished believe they are doing what they can to support those who are struggling, but they often see this work as a charitable opportunity for the virtuous among us to give of themselves to help the less fortunate. It is Christlike to help those in need, but after my service hours are up I return to the comforts of my White life. After all, it's *their* problem; I tried to help, but I can't do everything.

The project of this book stems from my role in Fordham University's Dorothy Day Center for Service and Justice. As the faculty director of the service-learning program for undergraduates, I worked alongside my social work and sociology colleagues to help students not only reach out to our local community but to analyze the conditions they encountered there. As a predominantly White institution in the poorest urban congressional district whose demographic is largely Latino and Black, the work of "good White Christians" revealed to me the challenges that solidarity and Christian love poses. If good White Christians want to see changes in the world toward racial harmony, they must work for racial justice. Justice will not come from individual acts of charity but will require the transformation of our social structures. Transforming unjust social structures is not their problem alone, but ours together.

The first aim of this book is to link our present realities of disparity to the generational dispossession legislated in America's past, and to see the problem of racial disparity and racialized unrest as our problem. Within this broad project a second aim is to trace the way Christian thought had a part in creating the racialized legislation by which people of color were dispossessed. As a Christian theologian whose primary area of research has been how Christian theology has thought about people of other faiths, I am interested in calling to task not only good White Christians in seeing our role in creating the conditions of dispossession, but also calling to task good White theologians to see our role in creating the narratives that made this dispossession seem reasonable, even ordained by God. The most lofty aim of the book is to rethink Christian symbolism that might guide good White Christians and perhaps others in undoing the sins of the past and contributing to a world of racial justice.

There are, no doubt, limits to my work. I am a White theologian inhabiting a "white habitus."[1] I was raised in a White

---

[1] Eduardo Bonilla-Silva, *Racism without Racists: Color-Blind Racism and the Persistence of Racial Inequality in the United States,* 2nd ed. (Latham, MD: Rowman and Littlefield, 2006), 104. Bonilla-Silva

neighborhood, found my theological voice in a White church, and continue to experience the "spatial impacts" of racial separation.[2] Shaped too often by the racially homogenous networks of a predominantly White neighborhood and earning my living teaching at a predominantly White institution, most of my closest friendships, intimate relationships, and sustained theological conversations are among White people. The systematic theology thus produced runs the serious danger of all predominantly White projects that the interests of White people will overdetermine the results.

Despite the reality of racial separation that has shaped my life and my field, I hope for a world that facilitates an inbreaking of the kingdom of God, a world that moves eschatologically toward "racial reconciliation [as] a divine gift and promise, partially realized here on earth and of certain fulfillment in a time known only to God."[3] This world will be one where my neighbors of color in adjacent towns have schools their kids are excited to attend or where our children go to school together. It is a world where economic security brings safety, maintained homes, and green space that are not determined by the boundaries of our neighborhoods and our race. This would be a world in which the community that surrounds my workplace is not shut out by iron gates, and a world in which those of us within the gates do not feel safer surrounded by them. This would be a world where bodily security, health, and recreation are equally accessible to all, a world where I can truly love my neighbor as myself. The project of this book is fundamentally a project aimed at cultivating love. And as James Cone has expressed, "Love in society is named justice."[4]

---

describes a white habitus as "a racialized socialization process that *conditions* and *creates* whites' racial taste, perceptions, feelings, and emotions and their views on racial matters."

[2] Joe R. Feagin, *The White Racial Frame: Centuries of Racial Framing and Counter-Framing* (New York: Routledge, 2010), 2.

[3] Bryan Massingale, *Racial Justice and the Catholic Church* (Maryknoll, NY: Orbis Books, 2010), 128.

[4] James Cone, *The Cross and the Lynching Tree* (Maryknoll, NY: Orbis Books, 2011), 71.

While I do this work as a White theologian, recognizing the limits of my abilities due to the White habitus I inhabit, I am indebted to my colleagues in the Dorothy Day Center for accompanying me in the antiracist work that also shapes this project. Many years ago my mentor, Sandra Lobo, recognized that the work of Fordham's Dorothy Day Center connecting a predominantly White institution with the concerns and struggles of a community of color could not be done without antiracist tools. She insisted that our work be structured through the antiracist training of the People's Institute for Survival and Beyond and its Undoing Racism workshops. My colleagues in the service-learning program have thus offered the most transformative relationships that have supported the theological thinking of this book. I am indebted to Justin Freitas, trainer with the People's Institute, Katheryn Crawford, Betamia Coronel, Kate Cavanagh, and Melissa Alvarenga for shaping so much of what I express in this book. I could also not have seen clearly the historical and structural realities of our national landscape as they played out in our local community without the analysis provided by Greg Jost. This book is dedicated to these colleagues and their irreversible impact.

The book is also dedicated to my children, Owen, Ella, and Thea. Like Martin Luther King, Jr., I too have a dream that my children will grow up into a world with greater racial justice than the one they inherited. To be honest, though, I think it might be more realistic to dedicate this book to *their* children (the grandchildren I do not yet know), given that this modest contribution to our world forecasts the long way we still have to go to enact structural change.

I am indebted to the Louisville Institute for the production of this book. A sabbatical grant for researchers given to me for the 2015–16 academic year allowed me the time to put the learning I had done with service-learning into the theological key that is my discipline. That year of writing, and all of my scholarly endeavors, have been first and foremost supported by Fordham

University. I am grateful to the institution and to my wonderful departmental colleagues.

I am grateful also for the companionship of my colleagues in the Northwest Bronx Community and Clergy Coalition, a grass-roots organizing body whose multi-generational, multi-racial, and multi-religious work has profoundly shaped my faith that our world can change toward justice. And I am grateful for the companionship of my husband, Michael Fletcher, who has been constant and patient with my learning how to love in our family, in our church, in our world, and in the writing of this book.

1

HOW CHRISTIAN SUPREMACY GAVE
BIRTH TO WHITE SUPREMACY

IN 1878, ON THE FLOOR of the United States Senate, Senator
A. A. Sargent rolled out a plan to ban immigration to the United
States from China. This came at a time when the Chinese had
already arrived in large numbers on America's West Coast, help-
ing to settle the land recently under US control and connecting
this new part of the nation to the old through their work on the
transcontinental railroad. Since the United States was welcoming
waves of immigrants from other parts of the globe to continue
to build the nation through new industries, Sargent's restrictive
proposal required some rationale. His argument was that by their
customs, their way of life, and their religion, the Chinese could
not be assimilated into a White Christian nation. His plan was
that Christian missionaries travel to China and "wash their robes
and make them white in the blood of the Lamb."[1] Then, being fit
for citizenship, the Chinese might apply.

Looking back on this historical episode, we might wonder how
such theological ideas, manufactured in "religious" spaces, had
the power to inform rights and legislation in the secular realm.
But embedded in this particular case is the further question of

---

[1] Aaron Augustus Sargent, "Chinese Immigration. Speech of Hon.
A. A. Sargent of California, in the Senate of the United States, March 7,
1878" (Washington DC, 1878), 23, http://sunsite.berkeley.edu.

how theologians manufactured ideas about Christianity and Whiteness that bound the two so tightly together. It was not just their robes that would be washed in the blood of the Lamb. Sargent's speech was part of a broader conversation about the viability of a nation and its future Whiteness, given the long-standing criteria that naturalization was reserved for free White persons. Sargent's argument and other immigration cases from his era demonstrate that Whiteness was a category that could be contested and that conversion to Christianity made people appear to be "more White." The criteria of Christianness featured favorably for a group of Syrian immigrants in the early twentieth century, when it helped their case for citizenship. Membership in the "Christian fold" served as a marker that they were part of the White race.[2] In another case from the same era Bhagat Singh Thind was recognized as Aryan and therefore Caucasian on the basis of linguistic and genealogical criteria, but his case for citizenship was overturned with the rationale that his "Hindu-ness" would render him unable to assimilate to White culture.[3] When the Chinese were categorized as non-Christian and non-White, it could be argued that they would compromise the thriving of a White Christian nation. Legislation passed in 1882 barred immigrants from China and later the Asiatic Zone. These restrictions were not fully lifted until 1965. The immigration debates of the late nineteenth century provide evidence of how religion and race

[2] Sarah Gualtieri, "Becoming 'White': Race, Religion, and the Foundations of Syrian/Lebanese Ethnicity in the United States," *Journal of American Ethnic History* 20, no. 4 (Summer 2001): 42. Gualtieri writes, "The sense of Christian entitlement to share in whiteness was markedly evident in the Dow case, which became a cause celebre for the Syrian immigrant elite in 1914."

[3] Jennifer Snow, "The Civilization of White Men: The Race of the Hindu in *United States v. Bhagat Singh Thind*," in *Race, Nation, and Religion in the Americas*, ed. Henry Goldschmidt and Elizabeth McAlister, 259–80 (Oxford: Oxford University Press, 2004). The Supreme Court case is accessible at http://www.bhagatsinghthind.com. We might note that the Christian lens painted others with broad (and inaccurate) brushes, as Thind was not Hindu but Sikh.

have functioned as twin imaginaries that have indelibly shaped the American landscape.

Yet, from this somewhat narrow focus, our lens might widen to consider these episodes as part of a more longstanding religio-racial project that has dominated in the ideology of a White Christian nation. The concept of a religio-racial project is an adaptation of the work of sociologists Michael Omi and Howard Winant, who have written extensively about America's "racial projects."[4] With the concept of racial project they show us that race is not a concrete or static reality, but an imaginative construct always created in particular times and places with specific material influences and impacts. Put simply, racial projects include the construction of racial categories (what the races are), the means by which persons are categorized into races (through physiological, biological, or phenotypical characteristics; ancestral country of origin; or other criteria that change over time), the meanings given to those racial categories, *and* the material benefits assigned or withheld on the basis of those racial categories. The history of the United States has been that of a White Christian nation in which the dominant racial project has been to create the category of White, sort some people into it, and assign material benefits on the basis of it to the exclusion of non-White others. The concept of racial *project* helps us to understand how the racial category of White has been dynamic and shifting, based on variable criteria at different moments in time. While much work has been done to trace the variety of racial projects that were enacted in the course of United States history (and its prehistory), only a little has been done asking the specific question of how *religion* functioned within these racial projects.[5] In expanding the concept to that of a religio-racial project, I want to draw attention to the way religion functions within racial projects. For

---

[4] Michael Omi and Howard Winant, *Racial Formation in the United States: From the 1960s to the 1990s*, 2nd ed. (New York: Routledge, 1994).

[5] See, for example, Goldschmidt and McAlister, *Race, Nation, and Religion in America*.

example, in seventeenth-century European encounters with First Nations people in Florida, Native peoples were named "red" and racialized on account of the body paint worn on sacred occasions.[6] In twenty-first-century accounts of racial dynamics in the United States, the term *Muslim* often functions as if it were a racial category rather than a religious one.[7] These examples give hints of the intersections of our conceptual categories of race and religion and thus ask us to consider the religio-racial project of any given moment. If Christianity functions intimately in the project of constructing Whiteness, Christian theologians should be especially concerned.

The religio-racial project of *our* moment is rightly the cause for much theological, political, and social concern.[8] Fifty years after the civil rights movement, our nation remains in turmoil not only in its racial project of Black and White, but new immigration since 1965 has created "the world's most religiously diverse nation."[9] While many commentators are concerned about a peaceful way forward, few have interrogated the ideology of White supremacy and its relationship to Christian supremacy

---

[6] Daniel Murphree, "Race and Religion on the Periphery: Disappointment and Missionization in the Spanish Floridas, 1566–1763," in Goldschmidt and McAlister, *Race, Nation, and Religion in the Americas*, 35–60.

[7] Simran Jeet Singh chronicles this contemporary religio-racial project in "Muslimophobia, Racialization, and Mistaken Identity: Understanding Anti-Sikh Hate Violence in a Post-9/11 America," in *Muhammad in the Digital Age*, ed. Ruqayya Yasmine Khan, 158–73 (Austin: University of Texas Press, 2015). See also Jaideep Singh, "A New American Apartheid: Racialized, Religious Minorities in the Post-9/11 Era" *Sikh Formations* 9, no. 2 (2013): 114–44.

[8] Jim Wallis, *America's Original Sin: Racism, White Privilege and the Bridge to a New America* (Grand Rapids, MI: Brazos, 2016); Robert Jones, *The End of White Christian America* (New York: Simon and Schuster, 2016).

[9] Diana Eck, *A New Religious America: How a Christian Country Became The World's Most Religiously Diverse Nation* (San Francisco: HarperSanFrancisco, 2001).

that is deeply embedded in our nation's history and our current landscape.

As we seek a way forward we must see how Whiteness and Christianness have been twin pillars of the dominant religio-racial project. Moreover, since the benefits assigned to those who inhabit the category of White Christian have been wide ranging, and the denial of benefits for those who fall outside the category have been death dealing, we need to interrogate the relationship of White supremacy and Christian identity. What this investigation will help us see is that the theology of Christian supremacy gave birth to the ideology of White supremacy, and that White supremacy grew from a dangerous ideology to an accepted subject position inherited by Whites. The systems and structures of White supremacy have been intimately joined with Christian supremacy, such that undoing White supremacy will also require relinquishing the ideologies and theologies of Christian supremacy.

To see the dominant religio-racial project of America as a White Christian nation requires that our scope be as broad as possible. While this will place limits on the depth of each episode examined, it will allow us to read a pattern in this history that might successfully be named an overarching religio-racial project of White Christian supremacy. Thus recognized and named, we can commit to the work of challenging this project and enacting alternatives in its place. If Christians desire a world of racial justice and religious integrity, understanding the sin of supremacy and theology's role within it is our only way forward.

SINS OF THE PAST: THEOLOGY'S ROLE IN BUILDING A WHITE CHRISTIAN NATION

In order to narrate the emergence of the United States as a White Christian nation, it is necessary to begin with the longer tradition of theologies of Christian supremacy. The Catholic Church, which blessed the imperial stretch of Spain and Portugal into the so-called New World, had long believed there was "no salvation outside the church."[10] This phrase served as a banner for Crusades as well as internal wars of religion, and it offered a rationale for explorers and conquistadors. One narrative posits that it was theologically unsophisticated conquistadors blinded by gold who enabled conquest to be propelled by ideologies of Christian supremacy. But the theological rationale ran much deeper and circulated more widely through authoritative spokespersons of the project of conquest and representatives of the Christian faith. Christopher Columbus explicitly wove the search for new lands and new wealth with a God-ordained destiny he saw prophesied in scripture.[11] With admiration for the endeavor of Columbus and his fleet, Pope Alexander VI affirmed that

> among other works well pleasing to the Divine Majesty and cherished of our heart, this assuredly ranks highest, that in our times especially the Catholic faith and the Christian religion be exalted and be everywhere increased and spread, that the health of souls be cared for and that barbarous nations be overthrown and brought to the faith itself.

The pope thereby adjudicated between Spain and Portugal that

> by the authority of Almighty God conferred upon us in blessed Peter and of the vicarship of Jesus Christ, which we

---

[10] Many trace the origins of this idiom to third-century bishop Cyprian of Carthage: "There can be no salvation to any except in the Church" (Cyprian, Bishop of Carthage, *Epistle* 61, in *The Ante-Nicene Fathers,* ed. Alexander Roberts and James Donaldson (Grand Rapids, MI: Eerdmans, 1952), 5:357). For an overview of how this axiom functioned in Christian history, see Francis Sullivan, *Salvation Outside the Church? Tracing the History of the Catholic Response* (Mahwah, NJ: Paulist Press, 1994); Jeannine Hill Fletcher, *Monopoly on Salvation? A Feminist Approach to Religious Pluralism* (New York: Continuum, 2005).

[11] See Saul Trinidad, "Christology, Conquista, Colonization," in *Faces of Jesus: Latin American Christologies,* ed. José Míguez Bonino, trans. Robert R. Barr (Maryknoll, NY: Orbis Books, 1983), 56.

hold on earth, do by tenor of these presents, should any of said islands have been found by your envoys and captains, give, grant, and assign to you and your heirs and successors, kings of Castile and Leon, forever, together with all their dominions, cities, camps, places, and villages, and all rights, jurisdictions, and appurtenances, all islands and mainlands found and to be found, discovered and to be discovered towards the west and south.[12]

A theology of God's plan for a Christian humanity ran from the pope through the field of faith formation and Christian theology. As Willie James Jennings describes, the theology of conquest was a sophisticated project informed by classically trained theologians. For example, when José de Acosta came to Peru in 1572, he was "thoroughly trained, intellectually accomplished, and doctrinally prepared." Jennings describes him as "a traditioned Christian intellectual of the highest order who precisely, powerfully and unrelentingly performed that tradition in the New World."[13] In Acosta's writing we can see "the inner coherence of traditioned Christian inquiry was grafted onto the inner coherence of colonialism," as the classically trained university theologians applied their training in the practical theology of conquest and colonialism formed by a partnership with Christian empire. Guided by an unshakable hermeneutic of Providence and a priori theological certainties, Acosta's systematic theology created a tight system into which Native peoples were fit and figured to be less than the Christian ideal. Similarly, in the preserved debates between Bartholomé de las Casas and the scholarly and legal

---

[12] Pope Alexander VI, *Inter Caetera* (May 4, 1493), *Encyclopedia Virginia*, transcribed from Frances Gardiner Davenport, ed., *European Treaties Bearing on the History of the United States and Its Dependencies to 1648* (Washington, DC: Carnegie Institution of Washington, 1917), 61–63.

[13] Willie James Jennings, *The Christian Imagination: Theology and the Origins of Race* (New Haven, CT: Yale University Press, 2010), 82, 68.

community in Europe we can see that it was the most skilled of theologians and scholars who shaped Christian thought and practices of domination and destruction of indigenous ways.[14] While disagreeing on the humanity of indigenous inhabitants, all sides in the debate agreed that God's plan included a Christian destiny for all peoples. This made Christians better representatives of God's will than any other people they might encounter.

Christian theologies of supremacy bound Christian identity across the denominational spectrum, and God's providence and plan provided the blueprint for colonization. Puritan Governor John Winthrop (d. 1649) of the Massachusetts Colony argued on the basis of Genesis 1:28 that God had given the land to "sonnes of men, with a general condition: increase & multiply, replenish the earth & subdue it," and since native inhabitants had not cultivated and "subdued" the land, God's plan could be rightly carried out only by Christian colonialists.[15] Thus, it was not only popes and princes, but Puritan governors who saw in the discovery of land outside of Europe a God-given plan for the expansion of Christendom. Architects of what would become the United States of America thought *theologically* about the project of building the nation, and they did so with remarkably consistent themes and often the best tools theology had to offer.

The struggle to establish what Winthrop called the "City on a Hill" incorporated patterns of thought that saw a Christian destiny for all humanity and distinguished those who were not Christian as both detrimental *and* instrumental in building the nation. Detrimental in that they might challenge the ideology and power of Christian nations; instrumental in that their bodies and their lives would be used for the work it would take to build the new nation. Through the theological lens of God's

---

[14] Bartholomé de las Casas, *An Account, Much Abbreviated, of the Destruction of the Indies*, trans. Andrew Hurley (Indianapolis: Hackett Publishing Company, 2003), xxxi–xxxiii.

[15] Eric Kades, "History and Interpretation of the Great Case of Johnson v. M'Intosh," *Faculty Publications (College of William and Mary Law School)*, Paper 50 (2001): 72.

design and the expectations of a hierarchy in humanity reflecting those who carry out God's design, European Christians surveyed the non-Christian other with disdain. This disdain hinged on the recognition of the person of Christ, enabling the distinction between Christian and non-Christian to serve as the value-laden opposition that is the cornerstone of Christian supremacy.

Just as classically trained theologians helped provide the logic for conquest in the so-called New World, in the early period of national formation the establishment of colleges was an essential strategy in expanding Christian domination. As Craig Wilder chronicles,

> Colleges were imperial instruments akin to armories and forts, a part of the colonial garrison with the specific responsibilities to train ministers and missionaries, convert indigenous peoples and soften cultural resistance, and extend European rule over foreign nations.[16]

It was in the academic spaces of theological training that ideas of Christian supremacy were manufactured as knowledge, to be put to the project of conquest, colonization, and conversion as they made their way from lecture hall to pulpit to legislative assemblies.

As the architects of a foundling nation struggled to extend Christendom, they employed their theological heritage to construct what will become a lasting dominant way of thinking, what Joe Feagin calls the "white racial frame." In Feagin's explanation, this long-term and persisting way of framing reality was created in the origins of the United States as a way of justifying the exploitation of non-White, non-Christian peoples during the era of land theft from Native peoples and labor theft by enslavement. The cosmology of a "great chain of being" functioned as a hierarchy with God, Christ, and Christians at the top, and the remainder of humanity hierarchically ordered below. Since

---

[16] Craig S. Wilder, *Ebony and Ivy: Race, Slavery, and the Troubled History of America's Universities* (New York: Bloomsbury, 2013), 33.

Christians were almost exclusively White, the sliding scale reflected this Whiteness. With a racial hierarchy as part of the natural order of things, non-White, non-Christian others were assessed to be deficient on a sliding scale of humanity, with the absence of Christianity the key determinant of greater and lesser humanity. At the same time White virtuousness was asserted in such a way as to protect the concrete interests of material gain that came as the result of unjust exploitation. In Feagin's words, "Each out group that was central to capital accumulation in Europe's colonizing expansion was denigrated."[17] Rationalizing conquest with theological tools, a White racial frame was constructed.

Christian supremacy had devastating effects on the Native peoples of the land that would become the United States, while it also provided the logic for enslaving non-Native peoples for the building of the nation. A longstanding Christian defense of slavery as biblically warranted was applied in new racialized ways. As David Whitford describes: "In the 1450s, Pope Nicholas V issued two bulls that linked West African slaving to evangelization. From that point forward, bringing 'Saracens, pagans, and other unbelievers or enemies of Christ' to the love of Christ through slavery was a popular justification of slavery."[18] The labor theft of enslavement was a crucial feature in the birth of White supremacy from the theology of Christian supremacy. The hierarchy of humanity with White Christians at the top reflected God's favor on virtuous human beings. If it was to Christians that God's favor was granted, non-Christians clearly had received the opposite in God's curse. If it was *White* Christians who demonstrated evidence of God's favor, Blackness could mark God's curse as well. The religious and the racial came together in the theo-logic of the "curse of Ham" that was mobilized by White Christians to justify enslaving Africans and employing their bodies in the

---

[17] Joe Feagin, *The White Racial Frame: Centuries of Racial Framing and Counter-Framing* (New York: Routledge, 2010), 39, 40.

[18] David Whitford, "A Calvinist Heritage to the 'Curse of Ham': Assessing the Accuracy of a Claim about Racial Subordination," *Church History and Religious Culture* 90, no. 1 (2010): 37.

building of a nation that would confirm God's gracious design. As Whitford states:

> As [a wide variety of late sixteenth-century and early seventeenth-century] authors manipulated and used Genesis 9 a clear pattern emerges, a Curse Matrix of interlocking tropes that gave the slave trade not only a justification but also a veneer of nobleness to the slave trader and owner. The Matrix consisted of three fundamental elements: 1) that black skin is the result of God's curse and is therefore a signal and sign of the African's cursedness to slavery; 2) that Africans embodied this cursed nature through hypersexuality and libidinousness; and 3) that these sinful and cursed Africans were also uncivilized brutes and heathens who were helped by slavery because they were exposed to culture and the saving Gospel of Jesus Christ. . . . This Matrix was then used for more than two centuries to repel any attack against the practice of African slavery in the English colonies of America.[19]

From out of this matrix emerged a theological pattern that repeated in Christian reasoning and Christian writing. First, God had a design, a Christian destiny for all humankind. Second, the sliding scale of humanity could be seen in God's favor on Christians and God's curse on non-Christians, reflected in skin and status. This logic informed a White Christian pattern of thought repeated throughout US history. An officer who chronicled sixteenth-century voyages used it with his speculation that "of this blacke & cursed *Chus* [son born to Noah's son Cham/ Ham] came all these blacke *Moores* which are in *Africa*."[20] An eighteenth-century judge in Boston reasoned with this logic to rule in favor of slavery on the assertion that Africans were rightly

---

[19] Ibid., 27.

[20] George Best, *A True Discourse of the Late Voyages of Discoverie for the Finding of a Passage to Cathaya* (London 1578), 31, cited in Whitford, "A Calvinist Heritage to the 'Curse of Ham,'" 28.

slaves because they were heathens, justly acquired as booty in wartime.[21] Nineteenth-century Bishop Auguste Martin of Louisiana defended slavery on Christian grounds seeing "slavery as an eminently Christian work . . . [in which] the redemption of millions of human beings who would pass in such a way from the darkest intellectual night to the sweet . . . light of the Gospel."[22] The theo-logic here rests on the singularity of God's plan for humanity and a sliding scale of humanity that allowed White Christians to argue themselves closer to God's favor and their non-White, non-Christian others deficient in God's eyes. This is what Feagin names the White racial frame—grounded in White virtuousness and assessing others to be deficient. But it was through theological reasoning of Christian supremacy that the White racial frame could be justified. Through a theological vision in imperialist settings White Christians placed themselves "in a God-position vis-à-vis decisions of eternal significance."[23] And God's eternal decision for humanity was marked on skin and reflected in status.

The persistence of the "curse of Ham" matrix and the solidifying of a White racial frame of virtuousness and assessment were not merely due to the internal logic of disinterested theologians caught up in theological speculations and scriptural cross-referencing. The production of theological symbolism and argumentation was undertaken by White Christians who had material investments in the exploitation of non-White peoples. As Wilder explains:

> The American college was an extension of merchant wealth.
> . . . Slaveholders became college presidents. The wealth of

---

[21] Whitford, "A Calvinist Heritage to the 'Curse of Ham,'" 32. The wider tradition of freeing baptized slaves (39–40) means that their paganism was one reason for continuing to enslave them.

[22] Bishop Martin, defending slavery, 1861, cited in Cyprian Davis, "God of Our Weary Years: Black Catholics in American Catholic History," in *Taking Down our Harps: Black Catholics in the United States*, ed. Diana Hayes and Cyprian Davis (Maryknoll, NY: Orbis Books, 1998), 25.

[23] Jennings, *The Christian Imagination*, 143.

the traders determined the locations and decided the fates of colonial schools. Profits from the sale and purchase of human beings paid for campuses and swelled college trusts.
. . .

Although half of the graduates of the earliest colleges became ministers, that fact had little impact upon the pattern of alumni slaveholding. Northeastern parishes routinely gave black people to ministers, and divines bought and sold human beings, distributed slaves in their wills, advertised for runaways, and sold people at auction.[24]

Once again, it is not uneducated individuals who unthinkingly applied theological arguments for their exploitative self-interest, but rather the most highly trained Christian theologians, ministers, university professors, and university presidents who manufactured knowledge that would become the ideology of White Christian supremacy. At the height of the slave trade to North America (1750–1810) knowledge systems were developed in the colleges that expounded theological systems of White supremacy. The knowledge of White Christian supremacy was useful when university presidents needed to sell human beings to keep their institutions afloat.[25] Through careful argumentation, theological formulas of Christian supremacy were standard reasoning. Describing the totalizing logic of Christian assessments of religious others, Jennings writes:

What is concealed in [the] formulaic articulation [of theologies of the religious other] is the centered white subject who discerns moral deficiency, salvific absence, and the eternal state after death. Colonialism is not the cause of this theological problem, but, bound to Enlightenment

---

[24] Wilder, *Ebony and Ivy*, 76–77, 85.
[25] Thomas Murphy, *Jesuit Slaveholding in Maryland 1717–1838* (New York: Routledge, 2001). For Murphy's treatment of the theological rationale of Thomas Mulledy, president of Georgetown, who sold 272 human beings in order to pay the university's debts, see 177–79.

reconfigurations of theological knowledge, surely is its refinement.[26]

Jennings's point here is that theological formulations never floated free of their White formulators. With the help of Enlightenment philosophy, social science, and "race science," Christian supremacy as White supremacy made logical sense. Here too, the production of this university knowledge was undertaken and informed by persons invested in the exploitation of colonialism. This ranged from influential seventeenth-century philosophers (like John Locke, who was an investor in the Royal Africa [slave-trading] Company)[27] to the slave-trading and slaveholding families who funded, founded, and served as presidents and professors in America's expanding university system.[28]

In the development of the university knowledge of White supremacy, the theology of Christian supremacy played a pivotal role as bedrock to the White racial frame. For example, even while Immanuel Kant rejected theological claims in favor of describing an architecture of universal humanity through reason, his philosophical system nonetheless employed the same theo-logic of a hierarchy of humanity pursuing a divine design. Taking Jesus as symbol for the human ideal, Kant saw a singular moral design, and subsequent moral favor and moral failing, enacted in humanity's diversity, reflected in culture, skin, and status. At Kant's historical moment the emergent sciences lent support to the application of these ideas. As Wilder reports, "This construction of the sciences [in the late eighteenth century] allowed humankind to have a single origin but varied progress; thus a contemporary racial hierarchy was consistent with a single genesis."[29] With a merging of science, philosophy, and religious myth, Kant was able to produce a theologically infused philosophy of humanity. Even as he rested his case on the criteria of Enlightenment

---

[26] Jennings, *The Christian Imagination*, 143.
[27] Feagin, *The White Racial Frame*, 156.
[28] See Wilder, *Ebony and Ivy*.
[29] Ibid., 226.

thought in the university setting, the theo-logic of White Christian supremacy was undeniable. With a single origin for humanity identified with Adam and Eve from the Genesis stories, Kant's religio-racial project saw four races emerging: "(1) the white race; (2) the Negro race; (3) the Hun race (Mongol or Kalmuck); and (4) the Hindu or Hindustani race."[30] All humanity shares a common origin, but it is the White race that Kant assessed as having developed closest to the original perfection of Adam and Eve. It was the White race, then, that exhibited a developmental progress toward perfection that exceeds that of other races. Aligning his reading of Christian myth with the emerging "race science," the White race stretches from Adam and Eve to perfection in Jesus Christ and anticipates "the perfect world order in which the ideal of the unity of the human species actualizes itself in the perfection of a race type, the white race."[31] As J. Kameron Carter has shown:

> [for Kant,] Christianity as rational religion and Christ as the "personified idea of the good principle" are the guarantee that whiteness, understood not merely and banally as pigment but as a structural-aesthetic order and as a sociopolitical arrangement, can and will be instantiated in the people who continue Christ's work, the work of Western civilization.[32]

The Christian theo-logic of the singularity of humanity tending toward the perfection of Christ expressed in Western culture and civilization allows for a judgment of some among humanity as falling short of the intended ideal and being deficient as a result. The striking conclusion Kant offers in his assessment of the non-White, non-Christian other is a compelling cautionary tale about

---

[30] Kant's 1775/1777 lectures on anthropology, cited in J. Kameron Carter, *Race: A Theological Account* (London: Oxford University Press, 2008), 84.

[31] Ibid., 81.

[32] Ibid., 89.

the power of university systems to mobilize evil. In his 1775 and 1777 lectures on anthropology, Kant taught:

1. The American[-Indian] people cannot be formed; they are not able to receive education. . . . They lack affect and passion. . . . They hardly ever speak. . . . They also care for nothing; and they are lazy.
2. The Negro Race . . . [is] full of affect and passion, quite vivacious, talkative and vain. They can be educated, but only to be a servant; that is to say, they can be trained.
3. The Hindus . . . are given to intense anger and to love. They can be trained to the highest degree, but only to the arts, not the sciences. . . . The Hindus always remain the same way; they will never make progress, even if they had gotten an earlier start in educating themselves.
4. The Race of Whites contains within itself all motivations and talents.[33]

The importance of Carter's study of Kant cannot be underestimated, for it demonstrates clearly the religio-racial project of arguably the most important thinker in the Western world's Enlightenment project. Kant's Enlightenment philosophy was subsequently used to underwrite modern theology from his day onward. His ideas were an important part of a dynamic mix in philosophical thinking. As Omi and Winant say: "By the time of the Enlightenment, a general awareness of race was pervasive, and most of the great philosophers of Europe, such as Hegel, Kant, Hume, and Locke, had issued virulently racist opinions."[34]

---

[33] In ibid., 91.

[34] Omi and Winant, *Racial Formation in the United States*, 63. For similar queries into the religio-racial project among eighteenth-century thinkers, see Gayatri Chakravorty Spivak, *Critique of Postcolonial Reason: Toward a History of the Vanishing Present* (Cambridge, MA: Harvard University Press, 1999); Kwok Pui Lan, "Beyond Pluralism," in

We need to hold in view not only the racist ideas that Kant promotes as philosophical insight, but also the widespread impact Kant had as a university professor, preeminent thinker, and widespread author, influencing the most respected sites within the education system from his day to our own.

This kind of thinking—religious justification that emerges from university education and racist/race sciences—was a link between Europe and the American context, where legislators, governors, and university presidents manufactured theological ideas consistent with White supremacy through the theo-logic of God's singular design for humanity best represented by the success of White Christians. As Wilder recounts:

> In a 1783 sermon celebrating the American Revolution, Yale president Ezra Stiles lauded the rise of the "whites" whose numerical growth alone proved divine favoritism toward the children of Europe. God intended the Americas for "a new enlargement of Japhet," the minister began, invoking the curse of Ham, and Europe's children were quickly filling the continents.
>
> It was "God's good providence," the president continued, that the vanishing of nonwhite people would also erase the moral problem of dispossession and enslavement. Breaking with a long theological tradition, Stiles applied the curse of Ham to Indians too: "I rather consider the American Indians as Canaanites." These were Noah's least fortunate descendants, and their destruction proved God's benevolence toward white people.[35]

Postcolonial Theory and Feminist Theology (Louisville, KY: Westminster John Knox Press, 2005); Jeorg Rieger, "Friedrich Schleiermacher," in *Empire and the Christian Tradition: New Readings of Classical Theologians*, ed. Kwok Pui Lan, Don H. Compier, and Joerg Rieger, 271–82 (Minneapolis: Fortress Press, 2007); David Kamitsuka, "G.W.F. Hegel," in Pui Lan, Compier, and Rieger, *Empire and the Christian Tradition*, 283–94.

[35] Wilder, *Ebony and Ivy*, 177. The curse of Ham was used often as justification for the enslavement of Black Africans. Identifying Ham as

God's designs for White people and White supremacy were manufactured in the academic spaces of theology and philosophy and
given a platform in the pulpit of university ministers and others.
Systems of philosophical and theological knowledge allowed
White supremacy to appear reasonable in the public square. But
it is crucial also to see this *symbolic capital* ultimately informing
arguments in the legislative sphere.[36] Christ's work of civilization and Christians perfecting God's call to "subdue the earth"
was such a powerful theo-logic that it circulated for more than
three hundred years. This theo-logic of Christian supremacy
underwrote manifest destiny in the White supremacist notions
of Senator Thomas Hart Benton on the floor of the US Senate as
he argued theologically for the annexation of Oregon territory:

> It would seem that the White race alone received the divine
> command, to subdue and replenish the earth! For it is the
> only race that has obeyed it—the only one that hunts out
> new and distant lands, and even a New World, to subdue
> and replenish. Starting from western Asia, taking Europe
> for their field, and the Sun for their guide, and leaving the
> Mongolians behind, they arrived after many ages, on the
> shores of the Atlantic, which they lit up with the lights of
> science and religion, and adorned with the useful and the

Noah's accursed son, sixteenth through eighteenth century biblical interpretation argued an etymological connection between Ham and Black,
rendering Ham as the accursed father of Black Africa. Contemporary
biblical scholarship finds no justification for this etymological connection. See David M. Goldenberg, *The Curse of Ham: Race and Slavery
in Early Judaism, Christianity, and Islam* (Princeton, NJ: Princeton
University Press, 2005), 149. Goldenberg writes, "The name Ham is not
related to the Hebrew or to any Semitic word meaning 'dark,' 'black,'
or 'heat,' or to the Egyptian word meaning 'Egypt.'"

[36] The concept of symbolic capital stands alongside other forms of
capital, including the economic capital of material resources (Feagin, *The
White Racial Frame*, 27). Just as economic capital provides for human
well-being as persons are able to purchase what they need for survival
and comfort, symbolic capital provides for well-being in the form of
ideas that affirm the value of persons.

elegant arts. Three and a half centuries ago, this race, in obedience to the great command arrived in the New World, and found new lands to subdue and replenish.[37]

Benton employs a theo-logic of Christian supremacy to affirm "this Christian people" of the White race replacing "the wigwam" and "the savages," moving across the land in a God-ordained drive to perfection that Christianity brings to the world. Only Whites follow God's design to subdue and replenish the earth; only Whites have and "bring" religion to the continent. With a sliding scale of humanity, others are made more perfect in the encounter with White Christians, where

> the Black and the Red races have often felt their ameliorating influence. The Yellow race, next to themselves in the scale of mental and moral excellence, and in the beauty of form, once their superiors in the useful and elegant arts, and in learning, and still respectable though stationary; this race cannot fail to receive a new impulse from the approach of the Whites.[38]

While we may be shocked by the clearly racist ideology that is propounded by legislators with an eye on extending US land and write them off as ideologues misusing Christian theology, it was the systems of theological production in university venues that made these ideas appear reasonable. Two examples—one fifteen years prior to Benton's speech and the other forty years later—provide us with some evidence that Benton could mobilize this symbolic capital in the legislative sphere only with the help of university systems of knowledge where theological thinking infused the disciplines.

---

[37] Thomas Hart Benton, "Speech of Mr. Benton of Missouri, In the Senate, May 28, 1846, On the Oregon Question," *The Congressional Globe* 29, no. 1 (1846): 918.

[38] Ibid.

The first example comes from James Kent, who in 1793 was the first law professor at Columbia College in New York City. After a distinguished career and still recognized as a leading thinker, he was asked to deliver the Phi Beta Kappa lecture during Yale's commencement in 1831. According to Wilder, Kent

> used science, theology, and history to proclaim the inevitable rise of the Europeans. It was the will of God that "the red men of the forest have been supplanted by a much nobler race of beings of European blood," he began. It would have been a sin and "a perversion of the duties and design of the human race" to permit "roving savages of the forest" to maintain these lands as "a savage and frightful desert."[39]

Note the theo-logic of God's design, carried out best by the Whiteness of a noble race of European blood and a hierarchy of humanity pursuing God's plan.

As the other bookend to Benton's racist speech on the Senate floor, former university president and prolific author Augustus J. Thébaud in 1881 argues theologically for the moral superiority of European Christians reflected in their status as global dominators. Thébaud proposes:

> The undeniable facts of oppression, invasion of rights, greed, and rapacity of some Christian nations in their colonies do not impair and weaken the truth that the present hegemony of the world by Europe was mainly the fruit of her superiority. . . . Europeans have acquired their present proud position in the world by their whole system of morals, still more than by their theoretical knowledge and universal culture. They brought to foreign nations principles of right, of justice, of humanity, of real benevolence, which were not known among them before, and which Europeans

---

[39] James Kent, "An Address Delivered at New Haven, Before the Phi Beta Kappa Society," September 13, 1831 (New Haven, CT: Hezekiah How, 1831), 14–15, cited in Wilder, *Ebony and Ivy*, 7.

themselves owed only to Christianity. . . . And it must be remarked that if the religion of Christ was to disappear at once from all the places where it sheds still its holy influence, all these proofs of a superior morality would also vanish at once.[40]

Like so many before him, Thébaud insists that the religion of Christ reflects a superior morality to other thought systems and religious traditions. This superior morality enables him to erase the undeniable facts of oppression, of which Thébaud himself is clearly aware. Here is the White racial frame at work, grounded in Christian virtue, elevating White cultural achievements, while erasing the evils of exploitation and extinction of non-White others perpetrated by White Christians. Thébaud's nearly five hundred page tome tracing the moral superiority of Christianity roots its argument in scriptural and theological evidence, moves through centuries and civilizations, and arrives at the nineteenth century's European encounter with the nations and religions of the world. Arguing against other scholarly appreciation of religious diversity of his day (for example, in conversation with William Lecky and Max Müller), Thébaud asserts that the moral superiority of Europe is owed exclusively to Christianity, rejecting concepts of "Moslem and Turkish benevolence."[41] That Thébaud argues against these scholars of religion demonstrates that there were scholarly options other than the sliding scale of humanity that placed Christians at the top. Thébaud, as a key player in an expanding US Catholic university system, chose not to produce and disseminate ideas of equality, but instead to participate in a religio-racial project of White Christian supremacy. Attitudes about the intersection of racial and religious superiority are evident in his theological defense. Thébaud writes:

---

[40] Augustus J. Thébaud, SJ, *The Church and the Moral World: Considerations on the Holiness of the Church* (New York: Benziger Brothers, 1881), 158–59.

[41] Ibid., 198.

> As to the pagan nations which [the Qur'an] has subdued, it
> must be said that in Africa, at least, it has *not* given many
> proofs of zeal for the destruction of fetichism [sic], most
> probably with a view to keeping on the Dark Continent a
> large supply of men eminently fitted for slavery, to which
> the Koran forbids to reduce "the believers."[42]

Simultaneously revealing an attitude that Africans *were* "fitted
for slavery" because of their religious practices *and* that it was
the fault of Muslim presence for enabling this so-called fetishism,
Thébaud reveals a complex entanglement of racial and religious
prejudice, developed and sustained by European (White) Christian supremacy and produced as knowledge in the nineteenth-
century university system.

Accompanying the disparagement of non-White, non-Christian
others was Thébaud's effort to mobilize university resources so
that other Christians be counted among the superior race of
Whiteness. In his major work *The Irish Race Past and Present*
(1873, with multiple editions over the next twenty-five years),
Thébaud attempts to lay out the sliding scale of humanity that
has been at work in the White racial frame and to ensure that
the (Catholic-Christian) Irish are counted at the top. Dedicat-
ing scholarly resources of time, expertise, and the backing of
an institution dedicated to educating White Catholics, Thébaud
proposes his project:

> There remains, therefore, but one thing to do: to consider
> each nation apart, and read its character in its history. Should
> this be done for all, the only practical philosophy of modern
> history would be written. For then we should have accom-
> plished morally for men what, in the physical order, zoolo-
> gists accomplish for the immense number of living beings
> which God has spread over the surface of the earth. They
> might be classified according to a certain order of the ascend-
> ing or descending moral scale. We could judge them rightly,

---

[42] Ibid., 200.

conformably with the standard of right or wrong, which is in the absolute possession of the Christian conscience.[43]

Similar to the driving thesis of *The Church and the Moral World*, Thébaud's point in these pages is to encourage his reader to "see how, from Christianity, the Caucasian race, as we call it, came to be the rulers of the world."[44] For Thébaud, the Irish were most close to an undisturbed form of Christianity and exemplified the ideal.

Noted intellectual and publicist Orestes Brownson reveals to us the impact of such scholarly production when he celebrates Thébaud's defense of (White) Irish cultural and moral supremacy as "a genuine book, solid and erudite, really profound and instructive, full of intense interest to many millions of American citizens, and of greatest value to the philosophy of history."[45] At a time when the Irish were struggling to secure their Whiteness, the symbolic capital of a university-theological system could go a long way. Simultaneously, as First Nations peoples were struggling to retain the little sovereignty that remained to them in the West, Thébaud's history of Native Americans (and their inability to lead a "settled life," as pagan and "degraded savage[s]") could have damaging effects.[46]

This brief sweep through three centuries provides evidence that at the deepest recesses of North American theo-logic is a pattern of thought that repeats itself, a theology of White supremacy that was manufactured within Christian university systems and that counted as knowledge. This pattern of thought is characterized by the theological ideas of God's singular plan, a Christian destiny for all, the value-laden opposition of Christian versus non-Christian, and a resultant hierarchy of humanity reflected

---

[43] Aug[ustus] J. Thébaud, *The Irish Race in the Past and the Present* (New York: D. Appleton and Company, 1874), vi.

[44] Ibid., 46.

[45] Orestes Brownson, "Review of the Irish Race in the Past and the Present," *Brownson's Quarterly Review* (1844–1875) (October 1, 1873).

[46] Augustus J. Thébaud, "The Native Tribes of North America and the Catholic Missions," *The Month and Catholic Review* 11 (1877): 147.

in skin and status. These are the features of Feagin's White racial frame, but it was theology that produced them. Through the ongoing production of theological ideas, the non-White, non-Christian other was situated on the sliding scale in such a way that Christian supremacy underwrote White supremacy. But, in the struggle between ideologies of White supremacy and ideologies of Christian supremacy, it was ultimately White supremacy that reigned. Even with conversion to Christianity, non-White Christians remained subordinate to the White Christian pinnacle of human progress. In fact, *White* Christianity defined Christianity itself. As Stephen Ray explains, "In the modern era, the ideas of Western and Christianity were framed as being over and against those who were totally other, who were *not* European, and who, most importantly, *were* heathens."[47] Ray continues:

> This particular framing establishes a new understanding of Western Christianity in which it is understood, on an implicit level, to be the natural religion of the European settlers over and against the heathen religion of the indigenous peoples and those who were forcibly indigenized to the Caribbean and other parts of the New World. . . . The common assumption in much of the North American context is that Christianity as a faith is most accurately rendered, discursively/culturally, as the faith of the West and its truest bearers are Western peoples.[48]

This ideology of Christianity as a White project and America as a White Christian nation was on display at the origins of the

---

[47] Stephen G. Ray, Jr., "Contending for the Cross: Black Theology and the Ghosts of Modernity," *Black Theology: An International Journal* 8 (April 2010): 59; emphases in original. The racialization of Native Americans as a religious project of Christian mission is outlined in Daniel Murphree, "Race and Religion on the Periphery: Disappointment and Missionization in the Spanish Floridas, 1566-1763," in Henry Goldschmidt and Elizabeth McAlister, eds., *Race, Nation, and Religion in America* (New York: Oxford University Press, 2004), 35–59.

[48] Ray, "Contending for the Cross," 59.

modern interfaith movement in Chicago at the 1893 World's Parliament of Religions. Here, the most prominent thinkers and leaders in the world's religions were expressly invited into a setting aimed to promote appreciation and cooperation among the religions, and yet American voices upheld the supremacy of White Christianity. Newspaper coverage of the event demonstrates another means by which ideas about Christian supremacy and White supremacy were circulated, both capturing and producing what's "in the air" in this historical moment. So, too, the published edition of the Parliamentary proceedings illuminate for us the worldview of the time and shaped its readers to inhabit that view of racial and religious difference authorized by the "experts." At the 1893 Parliament the most highly trained and widely respected scholars, theologians, ministers, and leaders were at home in the world of White Christian supremacy.

In his opening address to the assembly gathered in Chicago, Parliamentarian John Henry Barrows, chair of the general committee that organized the Parliament, acknowledged his Jewish collaborators as "men and women representing the most wonderful of all races," but he reserved accolades for the gathering as a *Christian* project undertaken distinctively in a Christian nation, asserting: "There is a true and noble sense in which America is a Christian nation . . . The world calls us, and we call ourselves, a Christian people. . . . and Christian America . . . welcomes to-day the earnest disciples of other faiths."[49] In Barrows's estimation, as an American project the Parliament needed to be seen as Christian.

For Henry Harris Jessup, founder of the American University in Beirut, the Christian project of North America was the divine

---

[49] John Henry Barrows, "Words of Welcome," in *The World's Parliament of Religions*, ed. John Henry Barrows (Chicago: Parliament Publishing Co., 1893), 1:74; also in Richard Hughes Seager, ed., *The Dawn of Religious Pluralism: Voices from the World's Parliament of Religions, 1893* (LaSalle, IL: Open Court Publishing, 1993), 25.

project destined for the Anglo-Saxon race.[50] In his address to the Parliament he expressed the wider sense of racial and religious manifest destiny that circulated in the late nineteenth century, proposing:

> There is a Divine plan in all human history. It embraces nations as well as individuals, and stretches on to the end of time. Every nation and people is part of the plan of God, who has set to each its bounds and its sphere of service to God and man. . . .
>
> But no nobler service has been given to any people, no nobler mission awaits any nation than that which God has given to those who speak the English tongue. . . . Was it an accident that North America fell to the lot of the Anglo-Saxon race, that vigorous Northern people of brain and brawn, of faith and courage, of order and liberty? Was it not the Divine preparation of a field for the planting and training of the freest, highest Christian civilization . . . ? This composite race of Norman Anglo-Saxon and Teutonic blood . . . of this marvelous continent, were sent here as a part of a far-reaching plan whose consummation will extend down through the ages.[51]

---

[50] Henry Harris Jessup and other speakers at the Parliament remind us of the prominence of the voices represented in this venue. As described by the Presbyterian Historical Society, Jessup was a graduate of Union Theological Seminary before years in service to mission in Syria. "In 1866, Jessup helped found the Syrian Protestant College, now the American University of Beirut" ("Biographical Note," http://www.history.pcusa.org).

[51] Henry Harris Jessup, "The Religious Mission of the English-Speaking Nations," in Seager, *The Dawn of Religious Pluralism*, 37–38. While Jessup's paper was not read until the thirteenth day of the seventeen-day Parliament, Seager selected this essay to open his chronicle of the event. It is remarkable that more discussion of the 1893 Parliament does not draw attention to the racist ideology of White Christians, given the scholarly reliance on Seager's work in representing the Parliament.

In welcoming the many representatives of the globe to the American Christian project of the World's Parliament of Religions, the Rev. Alexander McKenzie offered his opening remarks on the first day and invited the international delegates to see clearly the exceptional nature of the United States. Here, Christian citizens in their churches and schools have been "manufacturing a republic—taking the black material of humanity and building it up into noble men and women; taking the red material, wild with every savage instinct, and making it into respectable men."[52] For some, the Parliament's project fit within the wider religio-racial project of America as a White Christian nation that brought with it the possibility that non-White persons could be made noble and respectable through Christian efforts.[53]

Running through the history of the United States, from before its origins to the origins of the modern interfaith movement, the recurrent themes of Christian supremacy and White supremacy have been at work. The point in stretching this scope so widely and necessarily limiting its depth is to ask whether Christian-American theo-logic hasn't traded in the symbolic capital by which God's singular design for humanity and God's favor or curse are reflected in skin and status. As we see that this pattern repeats and functions in crucial legislative moments, we can attend to more historical episodes and fill out our framework with even more examples of this pattern at work. Analyzing the few gives us the pattern to follow as we analyze far more examples of symbolic capital of Christian supremacy underwriting White supremacy. Understanding the building blocks of the theo-logic and seeing its pattern repeat provide us with the pattern to look for in the new episodes we might uncover.

---

[52] The Rev. Alexander McKenzie, pastor of the Shepard Memorial Church, Cambridge, Massachusetts, in Barrows, *The World's Parliament of Religions*, 1:84.

[53] For a fuller discussion of the Parliament within America's religio-racial project, see Jeannine Hill Fletcher, "Warrants for Reconstruction: Christian Hegemony, White Supremacy," *Journal of Ecumenical Studies* 51, no. 1 (2016): 54–79.

The foregoing examples suggest that Christian supremacy and White supremacy have been the foundational logic of America as a White Christian nation over the last four hundred years. But this foundational logic does not simply fall from the sky. It is *produced* by those with the resources, interests, and positions to manufacture these ideas, build arguments that allow them to appear reasonable, and set them into the world as currency of symbolic capital.

Within each "world" of people living in the same location, systems of symbolic capital assign positive affirmations to those who rightly play their part in that world, while "glory, honor, credit, praise and fame" are denied to those whose bodies or practices are seen to deviate from the norm.[54] This symbolic capital is produced within families, by the state, and in educational and religious institutions.[55] Theology thus plays a crucial role in the comprehensive matrix of meanings by which persons are recognized as valuable, meaningful members of the collective—or are misidentified and relegated to its underside. At the intersection of the systems of education and religion, the university theologian is already an important figure in the manufacture of symbolic capital. When the power systems of education and religion have the capacity to influence the spheres of state and family, the theologian's role as benefactor and beneficiary of symbolic capital is unparalleled.

Modern race discourse in the Americas was influenced by the currents of symbolic capital from European philosophy, theology, and social science but took on its own agenda in the United States, where theology underwrote visions of White supremacy within university systems that were part of the building of a White Christian nation. As Wilder's study has demonstrated, in their earliest forms "colleges were imperial instruments" and the symbolic capital that flowed from these institutions was fed by the economic capital of wealthy merchants of the slave trade who served as "benefactors and guardians of colonial society."[56] In

---

[54] Mark Lewis Taylor, *The Theological and the Political: On the Weight of the World* (Minneapolis: Fortress Press, 2011), 88.

[55] Ibid., 39–40.

[56] Wilder, *Ebony and Ivy*, 33, 50.

the emergent institution of higher education in colonial America, many in leadership positions were also Christian ministers. The production of theologies that justified the enslavement of Africans and the destruction of Native peoples was a mainstay on colonial campuses.

As theological education systems produced the logic of White supremacy grounded in Christian supremacy, its influence was felt in other spheres because of the ways in which educational production, religious ideology, legislation by the state, and family values all coalesce as systems that produce value in the world. University theologians may be a particular site of power in having the time, resources, and material comforts to produce the symbolic capital of White Christian supremacy, but the reach of these ideas in influencing a much broader network through social interaction and legislation needs to be seen as well. In the production of symbolic capital there is a network of influence among theological ideas, public discourse, social outlook, and legislation. University theologians are responsible for much more than what they put into print on the page; they are responsible for the effects of what is produced as well.

SINS OF THE PRESENT:
WHERE DIFFERENCE MEANS DEFICIENT

This examination of historical examples of theology underwriting religio-racial supremacy is not only interesting historically but important from our present perspective insofar as these historical episodes had impact that reached beyond their moment in time. But, the patterns of the theo-logic of Christian supremacy are also important insofar as they might continue to function in the present. We may want to distance ourselves from the religio-racial ideologies that reigned in the sixteenth through nineteenth centuries for the dispossession of First Nations people, African Americans, and later Asians, Arabs, and Latinos in America. While US policies and social order may reflect transformed desires for the well-being of a great diversity of people in the context of the

United States, notions of White Christian supremacy still circulate. It is important to ask whether our discourses do not still trade in the symbolic capital of a toxic theo-logic of supremacy and assumptions that reveal a White racial frame.

I take the symbolic capital of my own traditions seriously when I ask whether a theo-logic of supremacy might continue to have negative impact upon people of color today in the current religio-racial project of a White Christian nation. While many herald the accomplishment of the Roman Catholic Church at Vatican II as opening a new way of being church in the modern world, especially in its openness to religious diversity, nevertheless, the fundamental logic of God's singular design for humanity, the value-laden opposition of Christian versus non-Christian and the sliding scale of humanity where some hold God's favor and others God's disdain still functions deeply as the theo-logic of the Catholic outlook. Is it possible that these theological ideas function as symbolic capital with the subsequent evaluation of persons measured in skin and status?

Commentators often celebrate the accomplishment of the Catholic Church when more than two thousand bishops gathered in Rome in the 1960s for a four-year long council, Vatican II. Here, they see an opening to a new era, especially in relation to the church's stance toward other faith traditions. When, for the better part of Catholic history the official stance was "outside the church no salvation," the documents of Vatican II do seem to say something new.[57] Responding to Vatican II's statement on non-Christian religions, *Nostra Aetate*, Pope Paul VI wrote that this document is evidence that "the Church is alive. . . . Here is the proof, here is the breath, the voice, the song, the Church lives.

---

[57] Contrast "outside the church no salvation" with "one is the community of all peoples, one their origin. . . . One also is their final goal, God" (*Nostra Aetate*, no. 1). For an overview of this shift, see Sullivan, *Salvation Outside the Church?* and Hill Fletcher, *Monopoly on Salvation?*

The Church thinks. The Church speaks. The Church grows."[58] Scholars since then will note Vatican II's "revolutionary character," when "for the first time in history, an ecumenical council spoke positively of other religions."[59] While speaking positively about other religions, nevertheless the theo-logic remains that God has a singular design for humanity, with Jesus Christ crucial in that design, and a sliding scale of humanity is evident in assessing whether or not people are carrying out God's design.

Repeatedly in the documents of the Catholic Church the idea of humanity's oneness is invoked, and this unity is part of God's singular design. Vatican II's *Lumen Gentium (Dogmatic Constitution on the Church)* states clearly that "in the beginning God made human nature one" (no. 13), and *Nostra Aetate* opens with the affirmation that "one is the community of all peoples, one their origin, for God made the whole human race to live over the face of the earth" (no. 1). Yet, within the unity of humanity there exists a graded diversity. For Catholic theo-logic this exists both within the church and beyond the church. *Lumen Gentium* offers a qualified equality among humanity, one that is comfortable with the idea of persons being of various "ranks."[60] In this theological anthropology, although God creates all humans equally, there is another force at work as the gifts of the Holy Spirit are bestowed in different ways "among the faithful of every rank" (no. 13). Some of these gifts are "outstanding" and "extraordinary," and others "more simple" (no. 13). Based on their

---

[58] Pope Paul VI, quoted in J. Oesterreicher, "The Declaration on non-Christian Religions," in *Commentary on the Documents of Vatican II,* vol. 3, ed. H. Vorgrimler, 1–154 (New York: Herder and Herder, 1968).

[59] Mary Boys, "What *Nostra Aetate* Inaugurated: A Conversion to the 'Providential Mystery of Otherness,'" *Theological Studies* 74 (2013): 73. A similar identification of this as a watershed moment is articulated by Ruben Mendoza (citing Dupuis, Knitter, Karkkainen, and Tanner), "Ray of Truth That Enlightens All': *Nostra Aetate* and Its Reception by the FABC," *Studies in Interreligious Dialogue* 16, no. 2 (2006): 148–72.

[60] A term used in paragraphs 11, 12, 13, 29, 40, 41.

affiliation and cooperation with Jesus Christ, humanity is seen now to form a graded diversity. In the words of *Lumen Gentium:*

> The apostles were *enriched* by Christ with a *special out-pouring of the Holy Spirit* coming upon them, and they passed on this spiritual gift to their helpers by the imposition of hands and it has been transmitted down to us in Episcopal consecration. (no. 21, emphasis added)

For Catholics, this means that the bishops are ranked in a higher order; indeed, through the outpouring of Jesus Christ they are seen as closer to divinity in a sliding scale of humanity when they are seen as "*presiding in place of God* over the flock" (no. 20). The result is a view of the Christian community explicitly employing ideas of supremacy and a graded diversity; there are ministers of "*lesser* rank" (no. 41) and "*lower* levels" (no. 29); others have "*supreme* power" (no. 22) and "*primacy over*" others (nos. 13, 18).

While for those within the Catholic Church this hierarchical conception of humanity might be disturbing enough, it is expressed in an even more expansive sense of a hierarchy in humanity when it is argued that Christians have supremacy over non-Christians. For example, within Catholic thinking there is an idea that the whole body of believers makes up the church and that there emerges a sense of the faithful *(sensus fidelium)* from the body as a whole. But, in articulating why that sense of the faithful is important, the value-laden opposition of Christian versus non-Christian comes sharply into view. As explained in the documents of Vatican II, "the body of the [Christian] faithful as a whole, anointed as they are by the Holy One, cannot err in matters of belief" (LG, no. 12). What this is saying is that Christians cannot be wrong in their belief when it is guaranteed by Christ. Even in the 2014 "*Sensus Fidei* in the Life of the Church" by the International Theological Commission of the Catholic Church this value-laden opposition and the guarantee of God's favor on the Christian sense of the faithful is explained this way:

As its name *(sensus)* indicates, it is akin rather to a natural, immediate and spontaneous reaction, and comparable to a vital instinct or a sort of "flair" by which the believer clings spontaneously to what conforms to the truth of faith and shuns what is contrary to it. The *sensus fidei fideili* is infallible in itself with regard to its object: the true faith. (no. 54)

In bridging the value-laden opposition between the human and the divine, the object of Christian faith in Christ renders the sense of the faithful *infallible*, thus guaranteeing that a Catholic's rank—however lowly within the church—is exalted and above those outside the church. Still, *Lumen Gentium* offers this caveat: "All the Church's children should remember that their exalted status is to be attributed not to their own merits but to the special grace of Christ" (no. 14). Affiliation with Christ results in God's favor on Christians. Christ is the cornerstone of Christian supremacy.

It is not only the Catholic tradition that claims Christ's supremacy (and therefore its own favor with God). In fact, some theologians argue that *all* Christians claim supremacy through the singularity of Jesus Christ in his role as savior of humankind. As Thomas Noble writes:

It appears that virtually the whole body of Christian theologians down through the centuries (with some exceptions) has held a common view. They are exclusivist in the sense that salvation is *a solo Christo* [by Christ alone], but inclusivist in believing that not all who are saved will be those who have explicitly put faith in Christ and been saved *sola fide* [by faith alone].[61]

Noble's claim is that "virtually the whole body of Christian theologians" has held the position that Christ alone is the bringer of

---

[61] Thomas Noble, "Only Exclusivism Will Do: Gavin D'Costa's Change of Mind," *Wesleyan Theological Review* 48, no. 1 (Spring 2013): 67.

salvation, that only through Christ do people access the culmination of God's plan for humanity. Noble's inclusivist position suggests that non-Christians can be saved anonymously by Christ's power, even if they are not saved by their faith in him *(sola fide)*. Noble concludes that there is a "firm Trinitarian base for a Christian theology of religions. That gives us the basis on which we may work out a position which holds firmly to the *exclusivism* of the *solus Christus* and holds a carefully modulated *inclusivism* with respect to the *sola fide*."[62] If Noble is right—that all Christians harbor a sense of singularity in Jesus as the sole way to salvation—a sense of supremacy in relation to non-Christian others is built into the faith.

Just as the medieval and early modern church functioned under the axiom that "outside the church there is no salvation," this position of exclusivism still lingers in the more recent inclusivism that is Noble's rendering: outside Christ there is no salvation (which is also the official stance of Catholic doctrine). Exclusivism and inclusivism share a theo-logic of God's singular design for humanity resting on Jesus Christ. What the exclusivist and inclusivist stances say is that apart from belief in Christ, one's life has no *ultimate* meaning (exclusivism), or that one's life falls short of recognizing the ultimate meaning of life God intends in Christ (inclusivism). Salvation, forecasted as a post-mortem event or this-worldly state of affairs hinges on the person of Christ. Conceptually, Christian theologians have argued that God's design in salvation and God's favor rests on those Christians who recognize and participate in the saving work of Christ. The result is a sliding scale of humanity, by which persons of other faiths are seen as less than their Christian counterparts. This strand of the tradition has functioned with the most damaging effects throughout world history since the ascendancy of Christian political powers and the expansion of Christian empires. As we've seen, this domination has been wielded against people of non-Christian traditions in the Americas, but it also functioned in Africa and in colonial contexts of Asia, as claims of Christian supremacy

---

[62] Ibid., 72.

propelled empires employing religious justification for political and material ends. And, it appears that it still functions today.

In the logic of Christian inclusivism, people of other faiths can enjoy some status on the sliding scale when their faith orientation reflects "a ray of that Truth" which is Jesus Christ (NA, no. 2). Insofar as the diverse wisdoms of the world's traditions approximate the truth of Christianity's true faith, the faith of the other is affirmed. Here is the logic of a pattern where what is different is deficient: the others are saved by their similitude and recognized as closer to the ideal by their relation to Christianity along a sliding scale. In the text of Vatican II's statement on religious diversity, Muslims rank close to Christian supremacy in their adoration of "the one God, living and subsisting in Himself; merciful and all-powerful, the Creator of heaven and earth." Muslims are assessed as worthy of recognition insofar as they "revere [Jesus] as a prophet. They also honor Mary, His virgin Mother" (no. 3).[63] Similarly, Jews might have a share in Christian supremacy because (so the document asserts) Christians and Jews share common fathers in the faith and God, as guarantor of supremacy, "holds the Jews most dear for the sake of their Fathers" (no. 4)—those fathers who have been claimed as common ancestors to Christians. The theo-logic of *Nostra Aetate* is that insofar as Muslims and Jews are *like* Christians, their religious traditions are to be valued, but the logic of Catholic teaching is that the fullest form of religious life is the Christian form. This is a sliding scale of humanity, rooted in the value-laden opposition of Christian versus non-Christian and exhibiting the same theo-logic that God's favor rests on Christians.

---

[63] For a compelling explanation of the Christian logic that affirms the first clause of the Islamic creed but not the second, see Daniel Madigan, "Jesus and Muhammad: The Sufficiency of Prophecy," in *Bearing the Word: Prophecy in Biblical and Qur'anic Perspective,* ed. Michael Ipgrave (London: Church House Publishing, 2005), 90–99. In the same volume Mahmoud Ayoub's "Isa and Jesus: Christ in Islamic Christology" offers an Islamic perspective on Jesus and important insights on the limitations of a Christian Christocentric view (87–89).

Christianity's elevated status may be distinctly a part of its theological project, but religious projects do not emerge free from entanglements in racial projects. If we press further to see whether *Nostra Aetate* hints at a racial project we might see one subtly embedded in its conception of culture. Affirmed positively, Buddhists and Hindus are among those religions that are "bound up with an advanced culture" (no. 2): Hinduism is valued for its "searching philosophical inquiry" and Buddhism for its teaching a way by which people might attain "supreme illumination" (no. 2). Both Hinduism and Buddhism are valued for their "refined concepts" and "more developed language" (no. 2). Yet, even as *Nostra Aetate* elevates religions connected with an "advanced culture," it suggests that there are those also entangled with cultures less advanced. Through a White racial frame the traditions of Christianity, Judaism, Islam, Buddhism, and Hinduism are named to draw a parallel between the achievements of Western culture and religion and the cultures and religions of these traditions. At the same time the religions of the dispossessed First Nations in America, African traditional religions, and the religions of the many indigenous communities overrun by Christian empire remain unnamed. Perhaps they are counted among the "various peoples" who exhibit a "profound religious sense," (no. 2), but the rhetorical distinction between peoples with a "profound religious sense" and those religions "bound up with an advanced culture" raises serious questions about whether the latter are the only ones to be accepted with true and holy elements. Situated as it is to culminate the paragraph on religions that are bound up with an advanced culture, the statement that "the Catholic Church rejects nothing that is true and holy in *these* religions" (no. 2, emphasis added) might be interpreted to affirm certain cultures on a sliding scale and marginalize further the religions of the dispossessed. In *Nostra Aetate* it is not the *races* of the world but the *religions* of the world that are the manifestations of God's singular, graded human diversity. But when religion is bound up with culture, and where Whiteness has been bound up with Christianity, the supremacy of Christianity too easily slips into a supremacy of White Christianity.

Christian supremacy entangled in cultural supremacy subtly conveys components of a racial project linking Christianity and Whiteness, while other subtle messaging happens in other ways. Although Christians don't generally see their devotion to Christ as part of a racial project, the work of Edward Blum and Paul Harvey invites us to consider how Christocentrism might have functioned in America at the time *Nostra Aetate* was issued in 1965. Using descriptions that were current in biblical scholarship, literary forms, and religious iconography, Blum and Harvey show how a Christ who was White had been increasingly asserted in the nineteenth and twentieth centuries.[64] In the 1960s, Warner Sallman's *Head of Christ* still reigned as the dominant image of a White Christ, mass produced and found in churches, seminaries, and households across the nation. A White Christ adorned Black and White churches alike, and although seeking to transcend race, even Martin Luther King, Jr., reinscribed a Christ who was White when asserting that "the Whiteness of his skin does not matter."[65] Albert Cleage preached the Black Christ as the heart of his ministry in Detroit in 1953, indicating the emergence of the consciousness that would become Black theology.[66] But at the issuance of *Nostra Aetate* and at the height of the civil rights movement the more widespread project of coloring the Christ had not taken root. James Cone had not yet published his transformative theology of the Black Christ, nor had Vine Deloria yet proposed that God is Red.[67] The Christ of *Nostra Aetate's* Christocentric theology may very well have appeared in

---

[64] Edward J. Blum and Paul Harvey, *The Color of Christ: The Son of God and the Saga of Race in America* (Chapel Hill: University of North Carolina Press, 2012).

[65] Ibid., 205.

[66] Ibid., 220–21.

[67] See James Cone, *Black Theology and Black Power* (Maryknoll, NY: Orbis Books, 1969), his first book. His presentation of the Black Christ is most fully articulated in *God of the Oppressed* (New York: Seabury, 1975). See also Vine Deloria, *God Is Red: A Native View of Religion* (New York: Putnam, 1973).

American Catholic minds as a White Christ. While *Nostra Aetate* is not explicitly racist in that it does not assert a White Christ, it is also not actively antiracist in challenging common cultural notions. In our own time we might ask ourselves what the dominant image of Jesus is as presented in our churches and press whether assumptions of White normativity and White supremacy aren't functioning still.

Late twentieth-century papal thought continued to exhibit notions of Christian supremacy and White cultural superiority. For example, in the 1998 document *Fides et Ratio*, John Paul II twice repeated the Christian supremacy of *Gaudium et Spes* that "only in the mystery of the incarnate Word does the mystery of man take on light" (nos. 12 and 60; see GS, no. 22). For this pope the Western cultural expression of the Word is essential. Pope John Paul II reiterated the pattern of God's plan for humanity embedded in Western civilization when he argued in *Fides et Ratio*:

> The Church cannot abandon what she has gained from her inculturation in the world of Greco-Latin thought. To reject this heritage would be to deny the providential plan of God who guides his Church down the paths of time and history. This criterion is valid for the Church in every age. (no. 72)

One final official teaching of the Catholic Church will set squarely in view the supremacist theo-logic that continues to be present in the Christian tradition. In 2000, with the publication of *Dominus Iesus,* a statement clarifying the Catholic-Christian outlook on the singular design of God for humanity and the sliding scale of humanity, resting on the work and person of Jesus Christ, Joseph Ratzinger (who would become Pope Benedict XVI), as prefect for the Congregation for the Doctrine of the Faith, wrote:

> With the coming of the Saviour Jesus Christ, God has willed that the Church founded by him be the instrument for the salvation of *all* humanity (cf. *Acts* 17:30–31). . . . If it is

true that the followers of other religions can receive divine grace, it is also certain that *objectively speaking* they are in a gravely deficient situation in comparison with those who, in the Church, have the fullness of the means of salvation. (no. 22)

Difference is not only deficient, it is "gravely deficient" in matters of salvific proportion.

Earlier I shared how the compelling work of Craig Wilder demonstrates that ideologies of White Christian supremacy constructed by theologians and university systems generated the symbolic capital on which the slave trade prospered. Theologians and preachers directly benefiting from the trade in human beings produced ideas that justified and supported slavery and White Christian supremacy. Universities that garnered land and capital from the dispossession of Native Peoples produced "knowledge" about the inferiority of Native Peoples.

The point of stretching the net widely across the many different points in the generation of symbolic capital is to note that the production of ideologies of supremacy cannot be traced to a singular origin. Yet, the repeated, pervasive, and "logical" presentation of ideologies of supremacy shapes the environment and has an impact on the lives of all who live within the network of social systems through which these ideas circulate. These persistent "teachings" of religious supremacy are transmitted as knowledge through university systems and have an impact on the ideas that circulate through the family and the state. What responsibility do Catholic theologians who repeat the magisterial teaching on the deficiency of religious others and Christian theologians who assert Christian supremacy in theologies of exclusivism, inclusivism, and the "new exclusivism" bear for the impact of these ideas?[68]

---

[68] Mara Brecht, "What's the Use of Exclusivism?" *Theological Studies* (2012): 53. There is also a range of contemporary theories defending exclusivism as epistemologically justified. See for example, Jeroen De Ridder, "Religious Exclusivism Unlimited," *Religious Studies* 47 (2011): 449–63.

Islamophobia, for example, is part of the reality in our moment, and the systems of symbolic capital fuel that reality. In a White Christian nation the environment continues to recognize White and Christian and to not recognize or to misrepresent others. Even today the White supremacy that emerges from Christian supremacy is death dealing for non-White, non-Christian others.

The charge that White supremacy is intimately linked to Christian supremacy means that Christian supremacy itself may be a problem. But, this charge of Christian supremacy runs deep, indeed to the very heart of Christian faith as Christians confess it. If we listen closely, we can recognize that the Nicene Creed, shared across the broad range of Christian denominations worldwide since the fourth century, harbors supremacist ideology. In the confession of Christian faith Christ is supreme above all others as Christians around the globe stake the claim in the second part of the creed:

> I believe in one Lord Jesus Christ,
> the Only Begotten Son of God,
> born of the Father before all ages.
> God from God, Light from Light,
> true God from true God,
> begotten, not made, consubstantial with the
>   Father;
> through him all things were made.
> For us men and for our salvation
> he came down from heaven,
> and by the Holy Spirit was incarnate of the
>   Virgin Mary,
> and became man.[69]

---

[69] United States Conference of Catholic Bishops, Catholic articulation of Nicene Creed. While a binding feature of many (most?) Christian communities, there are some differences in the way this portion of the creed is expressed. However, all of these expression include the value-laden opposition of "only begotten."

The words of the Nicene Creed have been named by theologians and scholars as the expression of Christian faith "that has the most widespread affirmation as definitive."[70] The creed is identified by some congregations as the key to "the unchanging faith of the Church,"[71] seeing this faith statement as an important crystallization of the right view of the Christian Bible.[72] In the words of David Maxwell, "When we confess our faith in the words of the creed, we are articulating the *fides quae* [the faith that is believed], the doctrinal content of our theology."[73]

Mark Chapman speculates that the creed may have been installed in Christian worship sometime in the fifth or sixth century as "an act of corporate reminding" of the theological position adopted by the Christian Church against other theological interpretations.[74] The creed was at times used by political rulers, underscoring

the political importance of unity and conformity: it was much easier to rule over a large area if everybody publicly declared faith in the same things—which, after all, is why Constantine summoned his council at Nicaea in 325 in the first place, and presumably why Charlemagne wanted people to affirm identical beliefs in the ninth century.[75]

---

[70] Winston Persaud, "Scripture, Creed, and Empire: Negotiating the Challenges to Find Norming Norms," *Dialog: A Journal of Theology* 54, no. 1 (Spring 2015): 74.

[71] *Confessing the One Faith*, rev. ed. (Eugene, OR: Wipf and Stock, 2010), xxiv, cited in Persaud, "Scripture, Creed, and Empire," 75.

[72] See, for example, George Parsenios, "The Creed: The Symbol of the Faith," *Theology Today* 67 (2011): 391–404.

[73] David R. Maxwell, "The Nicene Creed in the Church," *Concordia Journal* (January 2015): 13.

[74] Mark D. Chapman, "Why Do We Still Recite the Nicene Creed at the Eucharist?" *Anglican Theological Review* 87, no. 2 (January 2005): 209.

[75] Ibid., 210.

While theological interpretations of Christian tradition have taken an infinite number of expressions, the articulation of the creed functions (for some) as the grounding logic within which Christian thought is expressed. The expression of the creed binds Christian communities across time and space and is as close as we might come to a universal logic shared by Christians. But this universally leaning creed harbors a supremacist ideology in its expression, embedded in the relationship of Jesus to God as "only begotten."

In order to engage the supremacist ideology in the creed, we can begin with the first part of the creedal confession:

> I believe in one God,
> the Father almighty,
> maker of heaven and earth,
> of all things visible and invisible.

This first part of the creed insists on the unity of the created world, with God as the origin. The subsequent Christian logic is that all of humanity, as part of the created world, was made by God, maker of heaven and earth and of all visible and invisible things. The basic logic of Christian theology rests on the unity of creation and the unity of humanity; there is a basic equality, then, in the singular unity of the created world.

God is creator of heaven *and* earth, but heaven and earth are value-laden oppositions. In the second part of the creed, quoted above, we see that Christian tradition asserts that Jesus plays a special role within this value-laden opposition. Like humanity, he "became man," but Christ bridges the value-laden oppositions of heaven-earth and divinity-humanity with the assertion of his status as begotten. As Maxwell remarks: "There is really one doctrine in particular that the Nicene Creed is intended to address: the divinity of Christ."[76] In the words of the creed the

---

[76] Maxwell, "The Nicene Creed in the Church," 14. We can see clearly the focus of the Nicene Creed compared to the earlier Apostles' Creed. The Nicene Creed adds, "the Only Begotten Son of God, / born of the

divinity of Christ is established through a value-laden opposition hinging on the idea of "only begotten." George Parsinios explains,

> To say that Jesus is the only begotten Son is to say that he has a unique relationship with the Father. . . . We see a distinction between what God creates and what he begets. He creates the world. He begets the Son. In other words, whatever one says about God—that he is immortal, without sin—is true of the Son as well. . . . Whatever makes the Father divine—being uncreated, being without sin, being beyond time—is also true of the Son. Such characteristics are what it means to be God, and these are as true of the Son and the Spirit as they are of the Father.[77]

As *only* begotten Son, Jesus holds a unique place in all of reality: all things may have been created by God, but Jesus is the only begotten Son. This unique relationship to God also forges a unique relationship to humanity insofar as Jesus "came down from heaven . . . for our salvation."

Jesus as both human and divine bridges the opposition of divinity and humanity in his very being and creates the conditions for others to bridge that opposition as well. And yet, his role as bridge between the value-laden opposition of divinity-humanity makes affiliation with Jesus such that some created persons are qualitatively different from others. The assertion of value-laden opposition and Christ's role in bridging it, then, necessitates a hierarchy of some among humanity closer to the divine side of the opposition than others. Christ as singular event of perfection on the human side of the value-laden opposition requires that evidence of diversity among the human family be hierarchically assessed in relation to the singular norm, Jesus Christ.

Father before all ages. / God from God, Light from Light, / true God from true God, / begotten, not made, consubstantial with the Father; / through him all things were made."

[77] Parsenios, "The Creed," 398–99.

The structure of the Christian theo-logic rests in this dynamic of a singular unity of the created world, the oppositional distinction of Jesus as *only begotten* and "for our salvation," and a resultant hierarchy within humanity, where difference means deficient. This theo-logic played a crucial role in underwriting the White Christian response to non-White, non-Christian others. As we turn to the next chapter and explore the *material* outcomes of the ideologies of White Christian supremacy, we might hold in our minds the question of whether we can relinquish the grip of Christian supremacy in order to undo the damage of White supremacy.

2

THE WITCHCRAFT OF WHITE SUPREMACY

WITH A LONG VIEW ON the way religious themes have functioned in America's discourse of racial difference, the preceding
chapter called us to see the role Christian theologians have played
in giving birth to ideologies of White supremacy. Rather than
an anomaly in the theological discipline, the White racial frame
has been a dominant theological outlook by which non-White,
non-Christian persons have been assessed along a hierarchy of
humanity. Produced by persons who had a stake in the material
outcomes of White supremacy, university theologians traded in
the currency of symbolic capital so that Christian supremacy gave
way to White supremacy.

But what *are* the material outcomes of White Christian supremacy? In American history a crucial link has been forged
between White Christian supremacy as theology and White
Christian supremacy as subject position and structural reality.
This is because as symbolic capital assigns values of greater and
lesser worth to persons, it also functions as the logic by which
material resources are distributed. In the history of this nation the
ideology of White Christian supremacy generated by theologians
informed the legislative domain of the state so that the resources
of society were unequally distributed to benefit Whites. These
resources created the conditions for Whites to inhabit and inherit
social positions that were "superior" to non-White others. Claiming a priority for Christians, the practice and policy in the United

States since its inception have been to build a White Christian nation. Further, as Joseph Barndt has charted, "every institution in the United States—including every church—was created with a mission and purpose to serve white people exclusively."[1] These institutions were the channels through which White well-being was secured over several hundred years, building up the economic and human capital that Whites experience today. The task of this chapter is to demonstrate how White Christianity bears responsibility for the racialized disparity in which we live.

In succeeding in the struggle to establish the superiority of White Christians over non-White, non-Christian others, the history of the United States can be successfully seen as conjuring the witchcraft of White supremacy. Here, James Perkinson's analysis helps to tell the story of American history.[2] Prior to the establishment of the United States as a White Christian nation, the geographical area that would become America was populated by thriving cultures and peoples who were shaped in a sociality of relatedness to one another and relatedness to the earth. With the arrival of Europeans, White Christian supremacy may have been an ideology at work in the philosophies and theologies of Europe, but it was only an ideology. That is, it was an idea that held no currency in reality insofar as White Europeans actually struggled to maintain their bodily integrity—with the hazardous journey of sea crossing, the scarcity of food, and a lack of familiarity with the land and what it might produce for human sustenance. We can imagine that the first White Europeans on this continent struggled to secure their basic needs in a new land, a land that did not inherently privilege them; the supremacy of non-White ways may have been all too evident to them in their struggles. Even if an ideology of White Christian supremacy propelled Christian

---

[1] Joseph Barndt, *Becoming an Anti-Racist Church: Journeying Toward Wholeness* (Minneapolis: Fortress Press, 2001), 130.

[2] James W. Perkinson, "Reversing the Gaze: Constructing European Race Discourse as Modern Witchcraft Practice," *Journal of the American Academy of Religion* 72, no. 3 (2004): 603–29.

conquest and colonization, it would have met with a reality of struggle and uncertainty.[3]

Very soon in the founding of a new nation, however, White Christians began to establish their well-being by using the resources, bodies, and lives of others. Through their own "witchcraft," European Christians employed a mysterious and threatening potency that was the practice of using the other for their own gain. In Perkinson's description, through the projects of modern Christian empire "a 'witchery' of heretofore unimaginable potency ravaged African and aboriginal cultures."[4] From the first moments of colonial encounter, White Christians created the conditions of their superior subject position—with better access to resources, better housing, better education, better health—through the exploitation, extraction, and demonic control of others.

For Perkinson, the witchcraft of White supremacy was conjured through racial discourse as an ideological and practical frame that he identifies as "the quintessential witchery of modernity."[5] The race discourse of White European Christians named the other in such a way as to justify enslaving the other, exploiting the other, excluding the other, and establishing their own (White) supremacy. As Perkinson describes: "Early European race discourse can similarly be imagined as the mobilization of a curse."[6] We've seen that this race discourse was underwritten by Christian theology. Through the witchcraft of White supremacy American Christians mobilized this curse as a power that ate up Black, Brown, and Asian bodies to establish the superior subject position of Whites in a Christian nation. They did so through a variety of religio-racial projects that elevated Whiteness and

---

[3] For a challenge to the myth of European superiority in the context of conquest, see Matthew Restall, *Seven Myths of the Spanish Conquest* (Oxford: Oxford University Press, 2003), 131–46.

[4] Perkinson, "Reversing the Gaze," 612.

[5] Ibid., 614.

[6] Ibid., 620.

Christianness and devalued or destroyed others. It was White Christians who created America as a White Christian nation and through their decisions and legislation enacted the witchcraft of White supremacy. The religio-racial project of White Christians created the institutionalized racism of White supremacy that we can see in the disparity in evidence today. In Perkinson's chilling words, "Whiteness, under the veneer of its 'heavenly' pallor, is a great grinding witch tooth, sucking blood and tearing flesh without apology."[7] As we review the creation of the conditions of institutionalized racism, we might see clearly how White Christians created the conditions for their own supremacy.

CHRIST THE LIBERATOR AS DISPOSSESSOR OF THE PAGANS: FIRST NATIONS AND AMERICAN DISPOSSESSION

What I mean by White supremacy as a subject position and structural reality is the way in which, demographically speaking, the White population in America enjoys greater levels of economic stability, health, bodily well-being, and educational attainment than the non-White population. This stark reality of racialized disparity is one to which Christian theology must attend. But history can show us that it was White Christians, with the backing of theology, who created the conditions for this disparity and for White supremacy to be a structural reality.

Consider for a moment the experience of Native Americans in the United States. Statistically speaking, the measures of wellness in health, education, and economic security indicate that the indigenous peoples of this land are disproportionately compromised in their access to these fundamental rights. Keith Burich reports:

> The poverty rate among Indians is nearly 80 percent higher than the general population, with personal income nearly

---

[7] Ibid., 623.

70 percent lower. Ten of the 12 poorest counties in America are associated with reservations. Overall unemployment is nearly twice the national average, but that masks the nearly 90 percent unemployment rate on some reservations.[8]

And what is poverty's impact on health issues? It results in indigenous peoples experiencing a rate of diabetes that is twice as high as that for Whites, as well as a higher percentage of heart disease. Infant mortality is 60 percent higher than in the White population, and a suicide epidemic among young people on reservations indicates conditions that threaten Native peoples' lives. Fewer than half of the young people within the American Indian population finish high school, and disproportionately few are enrolled in and complete college.[9] The theological response of many Christians who are moved by this reality toward empathy and solidarity *might be* to bring Christ the liberator *to* Native peoples. But the history of dispossession of the original nations of this land is precisely a history in which Christ functioned to bring about the dispossession of the people.

The first moment of dispossession in US history is a moment in which Christ functioned as the distinguishing feature between those empowered with divine rights and those who would be dispossessed. The exploring nations of Europe abided by a shared pattern of Christian supremacy in determining who had the right to claim the land: if a Christian nation arrived and found another Christian nation already established, no rights to the land would be granted to the former because the latter already held title. But if a Christian nation arrived and found a non-Christian nation in the land, the right of occupancy held by Native peoples could be extinguished "by force or by purchase" by the Christian kings. It was Christians, then, who could secure individual rights to

---

[8] Keith Burich, "Murder by Poverty in Indian Country: Then and Now" *Indian Country Today* (March 17, 2016).

[9] See Center for Native American Youth at the Aspen Institute, "Fast Facts on Native American Youth and Indian Country."

the land, for example, in the 1629 Land Grant of King James I, which was directed "to all Christian peoples."[10]

Theological reasoning allowed Christians to keep non-Christian peoples from title to the land, because they saw Native peoples as having an inherent misunderstanding of human purpose. According to Governor Harvey (d.1646) in colonial Virginia, the Native peoples were "savages" having "only a general residency there, as wild beasts in the forest."[11] As we've seen, this resonated with Governor Winthrop of the Massachusetts Colony, who argued on the basis of Genesis 1:28 that God had given the land to "sonnes of men, with a general condition: increase & multiply, replenish the earth & subdue it." Since native inhabitants had not cultivated and "subdued" the land, God's plan could be rightly carried out only by Christian colonialists.[12] Religious justification found further resources in the emerging race sciences, as Chapter 1 has examined. Will Sarvis states:

> America was sparsely populated compared to Europe and rapidly became less populated with aborigines as a host of Old World diseases killed the immune-deficient New World peoples. Even before the multifarious pandemic began its grim course, the natives did not cultivate the land in the comparably intense way of Europe, lending further rationale for seizing property. The Indians were not Christians, thus an old European prejudice that had pitted Christians against Muslims for centuries came into play. European Christians used this same rationale to enslave non-Christians. Finally, the Native Americans looked different. With the rise of the race-based trans-Atlantic African slave trade,

---

[10] Will Sarvis, "Americans and Their Land: The Deep Roots of Property and Liberty," *Contemporary Review* (March 2008), 41.

[11] Eric Kades, "History and Interpretation of the Great Case of *Johnson v. M'Intosh*," *Faculty Publications (College of William and Mary Law School)*, paper 50 (2001): 72.

[12] Kades, "History and Interpretation of the Great Case of *Johnson v. M'Intosh*," 72.

skin colour and cultural differences gave the English and
Anglo-Americans an additional self-justification for taking
land from people unlike themselves.[13]

Theological justification cemented the European practice of
claiming land from Native peoples for the superior design of
God's plan. But an important moment comes when the claim of
Christian supremacy over Native nations was written into US
law in 1823. In this legislation a distinction was made between
the Natives' "right to occupancy" (as "heathens") and the "right
to title" (for any *Christian* people who had made a discovery
of the land). The ruling of this Supreme Court case *(Johnson v.
M'Intosh)* set the precedent "that the federal government would
not recognize private purchases of Indian land."[14] In making this
case Chief Justice John Marshall chronicled the common practice of Christian nations to assert the right to take possession of
lands, "notwithstanding the occupancy of the natives, who were
heathens, and at the same time admitting the prior title of any
Christian people who may have made a previous discovery."[15]
The practice Marshall cites was the protocol of the English, the
Spanish, the Portuguese, and the French. Marshall's opinion
reads, "While the different nations of Europe respected the right
of the natives as occupants, they asserted the ultimate dominion
to be in themselves. . . . The history of America from its discovery
to the present day proves, we think, the universal recognition
of these principles."[16] The principle Marshall summarized was
this: "discovery [by Christian nations] gave an exclusive right
to extinguish the Indian title of occupancy either by purchase or
by conquest."[17]

---

[13] Sarvis, "Americans and Their Land," 41.

[14] Kades, "History and Interpretation of the Great Case of *Johnson
v. M'Intosh*," 69.

[15] US Supreme Court, Johnson & Graham's Lessee v. McIntosh 21
U.S. (8 Wheat.) 543, 577 (1823).

[16] Ibid., 574.

[17] Ibid., 587.

An important point made by lawyer Steven Newcomb of the Indigenous Law Institute is that the fifteenth-century and sixteenth-century protocols and principles cited by Marshall explicitly state that while Christian peoples inhabiting a land could claim the right to own and sell land, the non-Christian, "pagan" inhabitants had no such rights—precisely because they were not Christian. While this was the practice in the fifteenth and sixteenth centuries, it was written into law in the nineteenth century through the *Johnson v. M'Intosh* case. Subsequently, from the nineteenth century to today, the right to land and sovereignty is traced through this case to the founding doctrine of discovery, namely, that Christian nations have rights to ownership by discovery that overrides non-Christian nations' right of occupancy.[18]

Claims about the supremacy of Christian ways of being in the world (namely, subduing the land and carrying out God's will in establishing Christian nations) translated into economic advantage that gave title and prosperity to Christians because land ownership formed the basis for the accumulation of wealth. From a strictly economic perspective, "the rule of *Johnson v. M'Intosh* ensured that Europeans would not transfer wealth to the tribes in the process of competing against each other to buy land."[19] It was Christians who could buy and sell land, passing it along through generations and establishing the economic conditions for White Christian well-being. Legislative decisions, built on the foundation of Christian supremacy, prioritized the well-being of Christians in building a White Christian nation and moving Native peoples onto smaller and smaller sites of land. The logic of Christian supremacy endured into the nineteenth century in the vision of American political leaders and presidents. As John Quincy Adams argued: "What is the right of the huntsman to the forest of a thousand miles over which he has accidentally ranged in quest of prey? Shall the fields and vallies, which a

---

[18] Steven Newcomb, *Pagans in the Promised Land* (Golden, CO: Fulcrum Publishing, 2008).

[19] Kades, "History and Interpretation of the Great Case of *Johnson v. M'Intosh*," 70.

beneficent God has formed to teem with the life of innumerable multitudes, be condemned to everlasting barrenness?"[20] And Governor William Henry Harrison displaced Native peoples with the same Christian logic: "Is one of the fairest portions of the globe to remain in a state of nature, the haunt of a few wretched savages, when it seems destined by the Creator to give support to a large population and to be the seat of civilization, of science and of true religion?"[21] White Christians built America as a White Christian nation, mobilizing the witness of the Creator to cram and crowd non-Christian, non-White peoples onto lands "reserved" for them.

When we look at the demographics of dispossession among Native peoples today, White Christians must come to terms with the foundational movements of White Christian well-being that removed health and prosperity from the original inhabitants of the land in order that the White Christian nation might prosper. The claims of Manifest Destiny and legal decisions that deny sovereignty to the original nations of this land rest on Christian arguments about inherent supremacy and God's design for the world. These claims created the conditions in which fewer and fewer resources of a rich geographical area would support the health and well-being of Native peoples, as more and more of those resources were dedicated to building up a White Christian nation.

Displacement of indigenous peoples from the lands east of the Mississippi, and greater and greater conquest of Native peoples made possible further gains for White Christians in the nineteenth century as the US government claimed title to more land and distributed benefits to its citizens. Annexing new territories, the United States now had a large geographic area that

---

[20] John Quincy Adams, 1802, cited in Ned Kaufman, *Place, Race, and Story: Essays on the Past and Future of Historic Preservation* (New York: Routledge, 2009), 374.

[21] William Henry Harrison, *Messages and Letters of William Henry Harrison*, Indiana Historical Collection (Indiana Historical Society, 1922), 492–93.

required the cultivation that God desired. Taking possession of Native land through purchase from other Christian nations, the United States now had land to give away to its citizens. But at this time naturalization was reserved for "free white persons" and citizenship defined by Whiteness.[22] Thus, in 1862, two important acts of legislation distributed the benefits of the newly acquired land exclusively to Whites. First, the Homestead Act gave 160 acres to "citizens and intended citizens" at a time when citizenship was limited to Whites; and second, the Morrill Land Grant Act made money available from the sale of land for states to establish universities that would build up US citizens. Through landownership and the empowerment of public education, the redistribution of wealth and resources from Native peoples to Christian peoples was a crucial shifting of balance to enhance the citizenry of America as a White Christian nation.

Citizens benefited from land and education, but Native peoples were not recognized as citizens until 1924; thus, the shifting of wealth and capital for some meant decreasing wealth and well-being for others. This historical shift affected the generational building up of wealth for White Christian citizens at the expense of non-Christian, non-White others. Christians must see the link between historical dispossessions and present disparities, and theologians repent of the ways Christian supremacy was a tool in this project. This repentance must include reparation, the priority of indigenous peoples' well-being, and the repudiation of the doctrine of discovery. Are Christian theologians willing to promote such changes?[23]

---

[22] From 1790 well into the twentieth century, the designation of free White persons as the basis of naturalization and citizenship was foundational. "The racial restriction on naturalized citizenship was not totally removed until 1952" (Erika Lee, "Immigrants and Immigration Law: A State of the Field Assessment," *Journal of American Ethnic History* 18 [Summer 1999]: 88).

[23] The governing bodies of several Christian denominations have repudiated the doctrine of discovery in recent years. While First Nations activists have met with Pope Francis (2016), no repudiation from the Roman Catholic Church has been forthcoming. Legally, the precedent

"MAKE THEM WHITE IN THE BLOOD OF THE LAMB"

Returning to the history of dispossession and tracing the witchcraft of White supremacy, we can see that claiming new land for the White Christian nation required bodies to cultivate the land. In the mid-nineteenth century, increasing resistance to enslaved labor meant that other laborers were needed. In addition to an influx of European Christians, invitations were sent out to Asian nations to send workers to fill America's need.

Returning to the discussion that opened this book, those invitations were well-received by many people from China and other Asian nations. Between 1848 and 1868, waves of Chinese immigrants came to the United States through California; by one estimate, in 1879 approximately 113,000 Chinese resided on the West Coast. Their status, however, was precarious. Erika Lee explains:

> Prior to 1875, then, immigration law was primarily under the jurisdiction of state governments. The one area of immigration law that the federal government controlled was naturalization. The country's first naturalization statute, the Naturalization Act of 1790, was at the same time extremely generous and highly restrictive. By providing that "free white persons" who had been in the United States for as little as two years could be naturalized by any American court, the act reflected Congress's confidence in the ability of European immigrants to assimilate and become worthy American citizens. By neglecting to include non-whites, however, the act established a racially encoded hierarchy of American citizenship that endured well until the mid-twentieth century. Until 1870, whether free blacks were citizens or not depended on which state they lived in. Native

---

set by the doctrine of discovery (a theological justification) continues to affect Native peoples in their struggles for sovereignty and land rights today.

Americans were considered members of "domestic dependent nations," or aliens who could not be naturalized.[24]

As America undertook its nation building on formerly Mexican land, states controlled the influx of immigrants prior to 1875, but naturalization into citizenship remained a benefit reserved for free White persons. Thus, Chinese labor was necessary for nation building, but a religio-racial project that defined them out of Whiteness denied them the prospect of citizenship in the nation they were building. As the number of immigrants increased, the White Christian nation began to respond negatively. Lee explains, "The move to restrict Chinese immigration in California began as early as 1855, but the federal government did not act until 1875."[25] Arguments against Chinese immigrants were economic (that they might take low wage jobs away from poor European immigrants), but they were also deeply informed by race prejudice. In Lee's words:

Explicit in the arguments for Chinese exclusion were several elements that would become the foundation of American gatekeeping ideology: *racializing* Chinese immigrants as permanently alien, threatening, and inferior on the basis of their race, culture, labor, and aberrant gender relations; *containing* the danger they represented by limiting economic and geographical mobility as well as barring them from naturalized citizenship through local, state, and federal laws and action; and lastly, *protecting* the nation from both further immigrant incursions and dangerous immigrants already in the United States by using the power of the state to legalize the modes and processes of exclusion, restriction, surveillance, and deportation.[26]

---

[24] Erika Lee, "Immigrants and Immigration Law," 87.

[25] Ibid., 89.

[26] Erika Lee, "The Chinese Exclusion Example: Race, Immigration, and American Gatekeeping, 1882–1924," *Journal of American Ethnic History* 21 (Spring 2002): 38.

Lee examines the gatekeeping function of American immigration policy in its racial and class-based exclusions, drawing connections between patterns of the racialization of other immigrant groups and the pattern of Chinese exclusion. Yet Lee does not indicate the way *religion* functioned as a criteria and how theology participated in this protection of White supremacy.

It was not only politicians but clergy as well who participated in the West Coast religio-racial project with public debates on immigration policy, as evidenced in the series of debates held in San Francisco in March 1873. James Bouchard, SJ—trained as both a Presbyterian minister and Jesuit Catholic priest—defended White interests when he insisted that the "immoral, vicious, pagan Chinese" were driving "good, honest [Christian] souls" into professions of ill repute when they take their jobs. His public lecture extolled the virtues of "the White race" and Christian morality against the "idolatrous, vicious, corrupt and pusillanimous" Chinese.[27] But, Bouchard was not the only theological voice in the immigration debate. The Rev. Otis Gibson publicly responded to Bouchard's propaganda and published a tract in defense of the Chinese. Yet, as a religio-racial project in a White Christian nation, even Gibson, a supporter of the Chinese could argue, "All invidious legislation should be repealed, and Christian men and women must multiply their efforts to uplift and Christianize these people."[28] To be American was to be Christian, and if

---

[27] James Bouchard, "Chinaman or White Man, Which?" *San Francisco Catholic Guardian*, March 1, 1873, cited in John Bernard McGloin, *Eloquent Indian: The Life of James Bouchard, California Jesuit* (Stanford, CA: Stanford University Press, 1949), 179. The complexity of Christian symbolic capital and the White racial frame mobilizing stereotypes for White interests is captured in the fact that Bouchard himself was of Native American ancestry and that the tickets sold for his public lecture were to support the school for White Catholic children in San Francisco.

[28] Rev. O. [Otis] Gibson, *Chinaman or White Man, Which?: A Reply to Father Buchard [sic], Delivered in Platt's Hall, San Francisco, Friday Evening, Mar. 14, 1873* (San Francisco: Alta California Printing House, 1873), 9, 13.

the Chinese could be Christianized, they might assimilate into a White Christian nation.

Such theological conceptualizations of the religio-racial other was not kept separate from venues of political decision making. As we have seen, this was the case when Senator A. A. Sargent argued for legal restrictions against the Chinese. Here is what he presented on the floor of the US Senate:

> The command of the Scripture is: "Go ye into all the world, and preach the gospel to every creature;" not overwhelm your own family, your own neighborhood, your own nation with the bigots and effects of heathenism. Let the missionary go to China and convert these men from their heathenish practices, wash their robes and make them white in the blood of the Lamb, and then, being fit for American citizenship and to become an integral part of our society, to be cemented into our political and moral structures, then let them come as immigrants. Until then, they deteriorate our body-politic and destroy our civilization.[29]

The thrust of Sargent's speech as a religio-racial project is captured in the phrase "make them white in the blood of the Lamb." This scriptural reference to the Book of Revelation takes on new meaning when the Whiteness that is proposed is a race category made possible by conversion to Christianity amid a history of violence.

As a religio-racial project of building a White Christian nation, theological voices and religious arguments were raised over many years to withhold the foundational benefit of citizenship from non-White, non-Christian others. But as scholars have demonstrated, at this point in US history, when Christianness and Whiteness were intimately intertwined, the non-White other

---

[29] Aaron Augustus Sargent, "Chinese Immigration. Speech of Hon. A. A. Sargent of California, in the Senate of the United States, March 7, 1878" (Washington DC, 1878), 23, http://sunsite.berkeley.edu.

could be "Whitened" through the process of Christianization.[30] Debates continued and policy decisions culminated in the 1882 Chinese Exclusion Act, which "prohibited the further immigration of Chinese laborers, allowed only a few select classes of Chinese immigrants to apply for admission, and affirmed the prohibition of naturalized citizenship on all Chinese immigrants."[31] Racist ideologies fueled the gatekeeping that protected America's sense of self, but ideologies of religious supremacy supported this work. As the debate continued over decades, racist ideologies continued to find a home in the US Senate; for example the Honorable George C. Perkins of California announced: "The Chinese are an undesirable class of people. This is the unprejudiced judgment of people who know them, after years of experience. . . . We would be much better off if they had never come among us, or if they would now go back again."[32]

In 1943 the United States repealed the Chinese Exclusion Act, but not without political resistance. In 1953, Senator Pat McCarran from Nevada stated before Congress: "I believe that this nation is the last hope of western civilization and if this oasis of the world shall be overrun, perverted, contaminated or destroyed, then the last flickering light of humanity will be extinguished."[33]

---

[30] Daniel B. Lee, "A Great Racial Commission: Religion and the Construction of White America," in *Race, Nation, and Religion in America,* ed. Henry Goldschmidt and Elizabeth McAlister, 85–110 (Oxford: Oxford University Press, 2004).

[31] Erika Lee, "Immigrants and Immigration Law," 90.

[32] Hon. George C. Perkins, "Chinese Exclusion. Speech in the Senate of the United States, Wednesday, November 1, 1893, on the Provisions of the New Chinese Law" (Washington, 1893), 9, http://sunsite.berkeley.edu.

[33] Pat McCarran, "Should Basic Changes Be Made in US Immigration Policy?" *Congressional Digest* (January 1, 1956), 19. Even today racist perspectives can be proposed on religious grounds. Liav Orgad and Theodore Ruthizer write: "In his controversial book *Who Are We?* Samuel Huntington called on Congress to adopt immigration criteria aimed at preserving the so-called Anglo-Protestant culture" (Liav Orgad and Theodore Ruthizer, "Race, Religion, and Nationality in Immigration Selection: 120 Years After," *Constitutional Commentary* 26 [2010]: 261).

In the rhetoric about Chinese others that spanned nearly seventy years, American Christians saw themselves as the ideal humans and religio-racial others as less than ideal and even less than human—but they could be made more human, more White and more American by their contact with Christians.

The exclusion of the non-Christian, non-White Chinese in the late nineteenth century expanded in the early twentieth century to exclude also immigrants from the Asiatic Zone, which stretched from the Arabian Peninsula to include a large portion of Asia and the Pacific Islands. Monumental restrictions on immigration strategically reinforced the idea of America as a White Christian nation when a quota system was put in place that privileged locations already represented in the US citizenry.[34] In this period arguments were regularly made that a group's or an individual's Christian identity brought it closer to the American ideal. In 1914, when a group of Syrians sought citizenship through the American court, they were granted citizenship in part because their "membership in the Christian fold" served as a marker that they were part of the Caucasian or White race.[35] Five years later,

---

[34] Chapter 185 of the Sixty-Eight Congress, Session 1, 1924, on the new immigration restrictions reads: "Section 11 (a) The annual quota of any nationality shall be 2 per centum of the number of foreign-born individuals of such nationality resident in continental United States as determined by the United States census of 1890, but the minimum quota of any nationality shall be 100." And "Section 11 (d) For the purpose of subdivisions (b) and (c) the term 'inhabitants in the continental United States in 1920' does not include (1) immigrants from the geographical areas specified in subdivision (c) of section 4 or their descendants [indicating no quota for the Western Hemisphere] (2) aliens ineligible to citizenship or their descendants [Asiatic Zone restriction of 1917 Immigration Act], (3) the descendants of slave immigrants, or (4) the descendants of American aborigines," http://www.legisworks.org/congress/68/publaw-139.pdf.

[35] Sarah Gualtieri, "Becoming 'White': Race, Religion, and the Foundations of Syrian/Lebanese Ethnicity in the United States," *Journal of American Ethnic History* 20, no. 4 (Summer 2001): 42. Gualtieri writes, "The sense of Christian entitlement to share in whiteness was markedly evident in the Dow case, which became a cause celebre for the Syrian immigrant elite in 1914."

as we noted in Chapter 1, Bhagat Singh Thind's case for citizenship was overturned on the basis that his "Hindu-ness" would render him incapable of assimilating to White culture.[36] From 1924 to 1965 immigration policies severely restricted and/or rejected the arrival of persons deemed unable to assimilate to the culture of the White Christian nation, including African, Asian, and Southern and Eastern European immigrants.[37] When the restrictive policies were finally addressed with legislation in 1965, they were recognized as racist in the words of Attorney General Robert Kennedy: "As we are working to remove the vestiges of racism from our public life, we cannot maintain racism as the cornerstone of our immigration laws."[38]

The 1965 immigration rules were very different from the pre-1965 rules. Whereas the mid-nineteenth century sought immigrants as workers in nation building, the mid-twentieth-century regulations gave preference to family unification and to "qualified immigrants who are members of the professions, or who because of their exceptional ability in the sciences or the arts will substantially benefit prospectively the national economy, cultural interests or welfare of the United States."[39] In this legislation a sliding

---

[36] Jennifer Snow, "The Civilization of White Men: The Race of the Hindu in *United States v. Bhagat Singh Thind*," in Goldschmidt and McAlister, *Race, Nation, and Religion in the Americas*, 259–80.

[37] Douglas S. Massey and Karen A. Pren, "Unintended Consequences of US Immigration Policy: Explaining the Post-1965 Surge from Latin America," *Population and Development Review* 38, no. 1 (March 2012): 1. Massey and Pren explain: "Countries of the Western Hemisphere had never been included in the national origins quotas, nor was the entry of their residents prohibited as that of Africans and Asians had been. . . . The 1965 amendments were intended to purge immigration law of its racist legacy by replacing the old quotas with a new system that allocated residence visas according to a neutral preference system based on family reunification and labor force needs."

[38] Cited in Diana Eck, *A New Religious America: How a "Christian Country" Has Become the World's Most Religiously Diverse Nation* (New York: HarperCollins, 2001), 7.

[39] "An Act to Amend the Immigration and Nationality Act," H.R. 2580, Public Law 89–236; 79 Stat. 911, 89th Congress, October 3, 1965, Section 3.203 (3), 913, http://library.uwb.edu.

scale of humanity is envisioned that no longer invites the poor huddled masses but prioritizes instead persons with "exceptional ability" who will help the nation to prosper economically and culturally. Those recruited and allowed to immigrate are already privileged by global flows of resources infusing their status and enhancing their well-being. This change in immigration policy might account for some of the data on Asian American populations showing that this group measures quite high on the criteria of wealth, homeownership, education, and health. If much of the Asian American population has arrived under the conditions of the post-1965 policies that prioritized professionals and skilled workers, these individuals and families had more resources that they brought with them from their home countries. These resources were not available to their Native American, Black, and Latino counterparts, but they appealed to the architects of a White Christian nation as a way of building up the country in a globalizing world. As William Vélez and Giovanni Burgos write: "Given a positive context of reception, immigrants with high levels of human capital can achieve upward mobility within one or two generations."[40] On measures of economic capital the story of Asian Americans may be a hopeful one. Yet the persistent presence of hate crimes against non-White, non-Christian populations and especially the rise of Islamophobia in the United States indicate that many Asian Americans and others from the so-called Asiatic Zone, while enjoying prosperity on the level of economic and material capital, still are threatened by the symbolic capital of a White Christian nation.[41]

---

[40] William Vélez and Giovanni Burgos, "The Imact of Housing Segregation and Structural Factors on the Socioeconomic Performance of Puerto Ricans in the United States," *CENTRO Journal* 23, no. 1 (Spring 2010): 181.

[41] See Simran Jeet Singh, "Muslimophobia, Racialization, and Mistaken Identity: Understanding Anti-Sikh Hate Violence in Post-9/11 America," in *Muhammad in the Post 9/11 Digital Age*, ed. Ruqayya Khan (Austin: University of Texas Press, 2015); and Jaideep Singh, "A New American Apartheid: Racialized, Religious Minorities in the post-9/11 Era," *Sikh Formations* 9, no. 2 (2013): 114–44.

SUPREMACY IN THE SENSE
OF THE FAITHFUL

Perhaps no demographic group in the United States reminds us more clearly of the ideology of America as a White Christian nation than the experience of many within the African American population. Enslavement is among the clearest examples of a religio-racial project in this White Christian nation, when the earliest arguments in support of slavery rested on the inferiority of non-Christian peoples. As the colonies established their own rules of governance, the distinction between Christian and non-Christian translated to the difference between enslavement and other forms of servitude. Note how the 1682 legislation in Virginia rests on the value-laden opposition "Christian" versus "non-Christian" when it categorized as slaves "all servants . . . who and whose parentage and native country are not Christian at the time of their first purchase."[42] From the seventeenth through the nineteenth centuries subsequent Christian arguments often invoked African paganism or Islamic inferiority on the African continent as theological justification for enslavement. The religio-racial project of slavery in a White Christian nation rested on the supremacy of Christianity in relation to non-Christian others.

This Christian supremacy was implicitly a form of White supremacy that came to see the emergent Black Christianities as derivative and therefore "less than" their White counterparts.[43] The truest bearers of Christianity were White, and White Christians maintained the value-laden opposition of Black-White in every historical epoch, even as Christianity grew among the Black population in America. In ecclesiastical and civil records

---

[42] William Waller Hening, ed., *The Statutes at Large; Being A Collection of All the Laws of Virginia, From the First Session of the Legislature, in the Year 1619*, vol. 2 (New York: Printed for the Editor, By R. & W. & G. Bartow, 1823), 491.

[43] Stephen Ray, "Contending for the Cross: Black Theology and the Ghosts of Modernity," *Black Theology* 8, no. 1 (April 2010): 53–68.

from Catholic Louisiana (in 1724) it was forbidden for pastors, priests, and missionaries to marry "white subjects" to "black."[44] In 1784, Spanish Catholic Florida's sacramental registers were kept separately for Blacks and Whites.[45] Extend from here to the long history of White Christian slaveholding among the Christian faithful: universities, seminaries, priests, bishops, and laity who possessed other human beings—even other Christians.[46] With emancipation, it was White Christian supremacy that often manifested itself in the lynch culture that terrorized African American citizens. As James Cone notes:

> The claim that whites had the right to control the black population through lynching and other extralegal forms of mob violence was grounded in the religious belief that America is a white nation called by God to bear witness to the superiority of "white over black." . . . It was the moral and Christian responsibility of white men to protect the purity of their race by any means necessary.[47]

It was White Christians who legislated and sustained the dispossession of Africans and African Americans on the basis of White morality and White Christian supremacy.

The sense of White supremacy among the Christian faithful was little diminished after the abolition of slavery, when reconstruction maintained separate spaces for the emancipated. Christian churches, schools, hospitals, orphanages, colleges, universities,

---

[44] "Civil and Ecclesiastical Records of Louisiana: The Code Noir, 1724," in *Stamped with the Image of God*, ed. Cyprian Davis and Jamie Phelps (Maryknoll, NY: Orbis Books, 2003), 9.

[45] "Ecclesiastical Records of St. Augustine Parish in Florida, 1796, 1812," in Davis and Phelps, *Stamped with the Image of God*, 5.

[46] Cyprian Davis, "God of Our Weary Years: Black Catholics in American Catholic History," in *Taking Down Our Harps: Black Catholics in the United States*, ed. Diana Hayes and Cyprian Davis, 17–48 (Maryknoll, NY: Orbis Books, 1998).

[47] James Cone, *The Cross and the Lynching Tree* (Maryknoll, NY: Orbis Books, 2011), 7–8.

and seminaries were segregated—a practice widely held long into the twentieth century.[48] Clerics in the Catholic Church continued to argue against the ordination of Black men on the basis that their status was "irregular because they are held in contempt by white people."[49] The contempt of White Christians for their Black sisters and brothers reveals a sliding scale of humanity at work. This sliding scale of humanity and White supremacy translated from an ideology to a subject position through the many ways that a White nation withheld well-being from African Americans. The refusal to educate, the resistance to full enfranchisement, and the regular practice of creating second-class citizenship generationally dispossessed Black Americans while securing benefits for Whites.

To connect present disparities to White Christian action, we might enter the intersecting systems of health, security, education, and economic status through the door of homeownership. An owned home is the single most important element in a wealth portfolio; it is the entry point for education, security, and health, and is the principle means by which wealth is transferred generationally. And yet, when the United States empowered its citizens with programs for owning homes, Black and Brown citizens were excluded from these benefits.

In the early twentieth century lending for homeownership came from three primary sources: life insurance companies, savings and loans institutions, and commercial banks.[50] These funding sources required a high down payment and a quick repayment plan, roughly six to eleven years. Under these conditions fewer

---

[48] Thomas Wyatt Turner, "A Letter to an Archbishop on the Situation of Black Catholics, 1919 and a Letter to the Bishops, 1932," in Davis and Phelps, *Stamped with the Image of God,* 91–93.

[49] Joseph Anciaux, "A Report to the Holy See on the Situation of African Americans in the United States, 1903," in Davis and Phelps, *Stamped with the Image of God,* 88.

[50] Matthew Chambers, Carlos Garriga, and Don Schlagenhauf, "The Post-War Boom in Homeownership: An Exercise in Quantitative History" (January 2011), 6.

than half of Americans were homeowners.[51] However, following the economic crisis of the Great Depression, Congress passed legislation that led to the establishment of the Federal Housing Administration (FHA). This "New Deal" legislation and the programs that followed enabled more Americans to buy homes with mortgages backed by the federal government, longer terms on the loan (twenty years to repay), and lower down payments. The FHA and later legislation providing Veterans Administration loans provided new opportunities for many US citizens to achieve homeownership, which served as a foundational source of economic stability and generational wealth. Between 1935 and 1965, homeownership increased from 48 percent to 63 percent, reaching a high in 2004 of nearly 70 percent.[52]

But, as in the past, access to these government-sponsored programs was racialized. In this case, it was the mortgage lending practices within the government programs that were biased by racialized (and racist) notions. As Douglas Massey and Nancy Denton have shown, "White Americans made a series of deliberate decisions to deny blacks access to urban housing markets and to reinforce their spatial segregation."[53] In the crucial period of

---

[51] "Prior to 1930, there was little federal involvement in housing except for land grants as exemplified by the 1862 Homestead Act. The Great Depression changed government's role in residential housing. As a result of the foreclosure problem that coincided with the 1929 collapse, Congress responded initially with Home Loan Bank Act of 1932. This Act brought thrift institutions under the federal regulation umbrella. The Home Owners Loan Act Bank (1933) and the 1934 National Housing Act were passed. These acts were designed to stabilize the financial system. The National Housing Act established the Federal Housing Administration (FHA), which introduced a government guarantee in hopes of spurring construction" (ibid., 7).

[52] Kathleen Howley, "US Homeownership Rates Falls to Lowest Levels Since the 1960s," *Bloomberg*, July 28, 2015; see also Chambers, Garriga, and Schlagenhauf, 26.

[53] Douglas Massey and Nancy Denton, *American Apartheid: Segregation and the Making of the Underclass* (Cambridge, MA: Harvard University Press, 1993), 19.

homeownership and equal opportunity throughout the twentieth century, White Americans systematically mobilized a racial project to exclude Black Americans from the generational benefits of homeownership.

Consider this passage from the appraisal manual used by the FHA (from roughly 1934 until at least 1951):

> Homer Hoyt, in his excellent book, *One Hundred Years of Land Values in Chicago* [1933], reports the results of a comprehensive survey of the infiltration of foreigners into that city, stating that the effect of racial and national movements upon Chicago land values was that certain racial groups, because of their lower economic status and standards of living, paid less rent themselves and caused a greater physical deterioration of property than groups higher in the social and economic scale. . . . Land values, according to Mr. Hoyt, in areas occupied by such classes are, therefore, invariably low.
>
> The classification that follows may be scientifically misleading from a standpoint of inherent racial characteristics, but Mr. Hoyt avers that it registers an opinion or prejudice that is reflected in land values. Likewise it represents the ranking of races and nationalities with respect to the beneficial effect on land values. Those nationalities and races having the most favorable influence come first in the list and those exerting detrimental effects come last:
>
> 1. English, Germans, Scotch, Irish and Scandinavians,
> 2. North Italians,
> 3. Bohemians or Czechs,
> 4. Poles,
> 5. Lithuanians,
> 6. Greeks,
> 7. Russians, Jews (lower class),
> 8. South Italians,
> 9. Negroes,
> 10. Mexicans.

No mention of Japanese and Chinese was made in the
above classification, probably because there were not very
large groups of Asians in Chicago at the time the survey
was made.[54]

The racial project of White supremacy is reflected in the production of knowledge of how race has beneficial and detrimental
effect on land value. But this racial project was also perpetuated
by the widespread use of this economic theory throughout the
systems that governed homeownership. Race-based assessment
of land value promoted the development of suburban areas that
were exclusively White and enabled restrictive covenants that
allowed individual homeowners to ensure the racial composi-
tion of their neighborhoods. The widespread practice of redlining, whereby banks and insurance companies color-coded areas
deemed hazardous due to non-White residents and withheld
loans and coverage, was driven by the racial project of White
supremacy and a hierarchy of humanity as it manifest in the
housing system.

We need not attribute any Christian motivation to the econo-
mists' work or trace any religious element in the real estate mar-
keters' arguments, but it was Christians who enforced the racial
hierarchy. For example, in the early twentieth century Catholics
had only recently moved into the White middle class, and they
were a first line of defense in maintaining the racial hierarchy in
housing. In the 1930s, Monsignor John Belford of Brooklyn reported, "Our people do not want the Negroes in the church, in
their homes, or their neighborhood."[55] As war efforts increased

---

[54] Stanley L. McMichael, *McMichael's Appraising Manual,* 4th ed.
(1951), 159–60, cited in Margalynne Armstrong, "Race and Property
Values in Entrenched Segregation," *Santa Clara Law Digital Commons,*
originally published in *University of Miami Law Review* 52, no. 1
(1997).

[55] John McGreevy, *Parish Boundaries: The Catholic Encounter with
Race in the Twentieth-Century Urban North* (Chicago: University of
Chicago Press, 1996), 55–56.

factory work and economic opportunities in the North, and southern African Americans sought relocation in large numbers in the 1940s, it was Christians and their priest-pastors who often lobbied against new government housing for the new Black population in order to maintain the position achieved by the White parish.[56] It was in a majority Catholic neighborhood outside Chicago in 1951 that Henry Clark rented an apartment for his family and was met with five- to six-thousand angry Whites who protested his act of racial integration until they were dispersed by the National Guard (the material culture of young women's crosses and young men's letterman jackets from Catholic high schools indicating Catholic resistance).[57] In northern cities, numerous priests in leadership positions mounted opposition to integration and enacted discrimination and harassment of African Americans, often on the basis of protecting White Catholic parish boundaries. In the 1960s, when northern cities again experienced significant increases in the African American population, Black families were not welcomed by White Christians.[58]

The participation of some White Christians in civil rights councils and demonstrations did not represent the whole of the Christian community, and at the height of the civil rights movement, when Martin Luther King marched through Chicago, Christian presence in the counter-demonstrations *against* King

---

[56] Ibid., 72–74.

[57] Ibid., 97. See also "Illinois: Segregationists in Cicero (1966)," *Eyes on the Prize: America's Civil Rights Movement 1954–1985*, http://www.pbs.org.

[58] The increase of African Americans in northern cities during this period includes Chicago's rise from 22.9 percent to 32.7 percent, Cleveland from 28.6 percent to 38.3 percent, and Detroit from 28.9 percent to 43.75 percent. Even cities with a smaller percentage of African Americans initially saw a rise in the African American population, as in Boston, which rose from 9.1 percent to 16.3 percent, Milwaukee from 8.4 percent to 14.7 percent, and Buffalo from 13.3 percent to 20.4 percent (McGreevy, *Parish Boundaries*, 180).

was evident. One eyewitness recounted seeing "people I went to church with, screaming 'Nigger!' and throwing rocks and dirt at King—these nice people I knew all my life. I couldn't believe it."[59] White supremacy was mobilized in the streets and in the churches:

> At St. Kevin's [Catholic parish] three African American Catholic women who dared attend Sunday mass found parishioners moving themselves away from the pews in which the women were seated. . . . Following one mass, crowds lining both sides of the steps leading to the church "hissed at . . . hooted at and assaulted" the terrified women as they walked to the rectory to pick up their church envelopes.[60]

The women recount being called names, "even during Mass. . . . When we went to the communion rail there were comments."[61]

What is important to recognize in the racist attitudes of White Christians is that the refusal to integrate schools and neighborhoods was an act of refusal of Black well-being institutionally and generationally. If homeownership and education create the conditions for economic security, but White Christians refused Black neighbors access to homes and schools, their refusal had not only social repercussions, but economic and material ones as well. The persistent reality of segregated neighborhoods even in the twenty-first century means that White Christians have not yet repented of the past sins of racial segregation and the sharing of symbolic and economic capital that this requires.

---

[59] Ibid., 190. McGreevy cites accounts of the Chicago demonstrations from Fr. James A. Bowman, SJ, letter to *Commonweal* 85 (December 16, 1966), 323; John A. McDermott, "A Chicago Catholic Asks: Where Does My Church Stand on Racial Justice?" *Look* (November 1, 1966), 80ff.; William Graney, "Saddest Part of Riot: 'Catholic' Know Nothings," *The New World* (August 5, 1966); Dennis Geaney, "Trouble in Chicago," *Ave Maria* 104 (October 1, 1966), 11.

[60] McGreevy, *Parish Boundaries*, 98.

[61] Ibid., 100.

LATINO AS RACIAL CATEGORY
AND THE BOUNDARIES OF WHITENESS

As evidenced in the foregoing episodes, the witchcraft of White supremacy fed on the bodies of others to produce a White Christian nation in which access to land, citizenship, and home-ownership was regularly reserved for Whites. As in the case of African American Christians, the history of Latino Americans also demonstrates a willingness of White Christians to feed on their co-Christian others. In the histories of the fifty-four million Latinos who make up 17 percent of the US population, we see again the witchcraft of White supremacy in the United States. In the words of Juan Gonzalez, we see "how bountiful our nation's promise has turned out for some, how needlessly heartbreaking for others."[62] While the particular stories of distinct Latino groups require attention to their specificity, there is a powerful statement of White supremacy when, despite the range of racial categories persons of Latin American origin inhabit, Latinos in America disproportionately suffer from economic insecurity, educational opportunity, and bodily integrity (in measure of health and safety) in comparison to their non-Latino White counterparts.[63]

Among the peculiarities of discussing the religio-racial project of a White Christian nation as it affects Latino Americans is the

---

[62] Juan Gonzalez, *Harvest of Empire: A History of Latinos in America*, rev. ed. (New York: Penguin, 2011), xxiii. Demographics on the US Latino population can be found on the US Census Bureau website, http://www.census.gov.

[63] According to the US Census Bureau, in 2015 "Hispanics constituted 17.6% of the nation's total population," and "24.3% of elementary and high school students. Also, "17.0% . . . of students (both undergraduate and graduate) enrolled in college in 2015 were Hispanic." "$45,150 [was] the median income of Hispanic households in 2015, while "21.4% was the poverty rate" (see "FFF: Hispanic Heritage Month 2016," release no. CB16–FF.16 [October 12, 2016], http://www.census.gov). For non-Hispanic Whites, the poverty rate was 9.1%, for Blacks 24.1%, and for Asians 11.3% ("Income and Poverty in the United States: 2015," report no. P60–256 [September 13, 2016], http://www.census.gov).

puzzling reality that Latino Americans are largely Christian and many are White. In the official categorization of the US Census, Latino (Hispanic) is not a race but an ethnicity. This means that the term encompasses a wide range of racial categories, reflecting the hybridity of racial projects in diverse Latin American countries. As Victor Rodríguez Domínguez states: "The racialization of people of Latin American origin (in particular Puerto Ricans and Mexican Americans) was also distinct from the racialization of others in the United States because emigrating Latinos came from countries where miscegenation was common and where the idea of *mestizaje* was part of nation-building efforts."[64]

While the racial projects of different Latin American countries result in diverse racial categories within the collective *Latino,* Latinos in America have historically faced the racial project of a Black-White binary. Many Latinos identify as White when these are the only two options, but the persistent dispossession of Latinos in America suggests that they find themselves in the United States within a particular racial project where *White* is marked by language and grounded in European supremacy. Thus, despite census categories that render *Latino (Hispanic)* not a race (but an ethnicity within which there are a multiplicity of races), a regular pattern of *racialization* has functionally created Latino as a category that reveals the impact of racism in exclusions from the benefits of a White Christian nation.[65]

For a case study to highlight this, we might look at the experience of Mexican Americans, the largest group of Latinos in America (64 percent of the total US Latino population). Mexican Americans were among the earliest Latino Americans

---

[64] Victor Rodríguez Domínguez, "The Racialization of Mexican Americans and Puerto Ricans: 1890s-1930s," *CENTRO Journal* 27, no. 1 (Spring 2005): 74. He points out that the category *mestizaje* in Mexico incorporated Mexicans of African descent.

[65] Despite the technicalities of census categorization, Joseph Barndt argues that "the enforced process of racialization in the United States created six main racial groups: Native American, African American, Latino/Hispanic, Asian American, Arab American, and white" (Barndt, *Becoming an Anti-Racist Church*, 134).

(in the nineteenth century), and yet they continue to experience exclusion and oppression today. As Gonzalez writes, "No Hispanic group has contributed more to the nation's prosperity than Mexicans, yet none makes white America more uneasy about the future."[66] In this history we see the White Christian nation again feeding on its others.

Soon after Latin American countries declared their independence from Spanish rule, the US government set its sights on involvement, control, and ultimately annexation of land from many new nations. Such was the case with Mexico. As Gonzalez explains, in the early years of Mexican independence

> the United States of Mexico, as the new country called itself, and the United States of America were eerily similar in territory and population. In 1824 Mexico comprised 1.7 million square miles and contained 6 million people, while the United States stretched for 1.8 million square miles and had 9.6 million people. That equivalence was radically transformed over the next three decades as Anglo settlers poured into Mexican land.[67]

With the help of race science and the theo-logic of Manifest Destiny, the United States of America expanded into the United States of Mexico between the years 1836 and 1853. Former residents of Mexico were granted American citizenship, but under the new governance of the United States of America, White settlers gained more and more control over Mexican American land. Key in this were structures and systems that gave English-speaking Whites an advantage. For example, an English-only court system favored Whites in a land rush that allowed White Americans to purchase "fraudulent squatters' titles and [outlast] the real Mexican owners in the courts."[68] The resulting dispossession of land is an important chapter in the witchcraft of White supremacy.

---

[66] Gonzalez, *Harvest of Empire*, 96.

[67] Ibid., 39.

[68] Ibid., 100.

In 1850, property in Texas had been pretty evenly divided between the two groups. That year, according to the US Census, *tejanos* [Spanish/Mexicans] comprised 32.4 percent of the workers in the state and owned 33 percent of its wealth. Over the next twenty years, however, things changed drastically. By 1870, *tejanos* were 47.6 percent of the workforce but possessed only 10.6 percent of the wealth.[69]

By the 1920s, the Rio Grande valley was divided: "Mexicans comprised more than 90 percent of its population, but the white minority controlled most of the land and all the political power."[70] The distinction between who owned the land and who worked the land is a critical, racialized distinction, one that connects with other rights in an interlocking system of education, wealth, health, and bodily security.

In the early years of US control of formerly Mexican land, Mexican Americans held a unique racial location because of their economic status and their religious identification, demonstrating again the role of Christianity in the U.S religio-racial project. As Victor Rodríguez Domínguez reports:

> In the racial hierarchy constructed by white settlers in the newly conquered southwest, Mexicans, because they were Christians and mestizos and still included a significant landed elite who mediated between Anglo whites and Mexicans, were not entirely racialized in the process. As a social group, Mexicans became an ethnic group akin to European immigrants, in the sense that the basic process of differentiation was rooted in culture, not race. During this period, the otherness of Mexicans was rooted in culture

---

[69] Ibid., 102. Gonzalez's source is Arnoldo De León, *Tejanos and the Numbers Game: A Socio-Historical Interpretation from the Federal Censuses, 1850–1900* (Albuquerque: University of New Mexico Press, 1989), 42–43.

[70] Gonzalez, *Harvest of Empire*, 102.

rather than in some assumed biological difference. This more biological racialization begins to occur at the end of the 19th century and is particularly powerful during the 20th century.[71]

As White populations grew in the American Southwest, Mexican Americans were squeezed out of political power and their racialization, as a non-White and inferior group, was mobilized with the help of growing literature of scientific racism and social Darwinism.[72] As was the case for African Americans, Christian love was less powerful than racist ideologies in the racial projects of America as a White Christian nation. Rodríguez Domínguez continues:

> By the end of the 19th century the United States had extended its imperial hegemony over Mexico while at the same time completing the subordination and racialization of Mexican Americans in the Southwest. The Mexicans, displaced by the dislocating forces of US capital in Mexico, ended up migrating into the racialized space of the Southwest. These newly arrived Mexicans constitute the material out of which a racialized Mexican American population was constructed.[73]

In the racial-project of late nineteenth century America, the Mexican's Christianness was trumped by a racialization of the Mexican as non-White.

Following this first phase of Mexican American presence in the United States, the United States continued its economic interests in Mexico. It inserted itself into Mexico's politics and economics in order to secure its own interests, at the expense of the citizens of Mexico. This shift in power intimately connected to "a series

---

[71] Rodríguez Domínguez, "The Racialization of Mexican American and Puerto Ricans," 76.
[72] Ibid., 77.
[73] Ibid., 82.

of military occupations early in the century [that] . . . allowed US banks and corporations to gain control over key industries in every country. Latin American ventures sprang up on Wall Street overnight as sugar, fruit, railroad, mining, gas, and electric company executives raced south on the heels of the marines."[74] The geographic proximity enabled Mexico and the United States to develop intimate economic ties, consistently benefiting the powerful interests of the United States. As the White Christian nation feeds on its Asian, Native, and African American others, it turns regularly to Mexican bodies when these others become unavailable. Juan Gonzalez describes this disposability of Mexican workers in America's interests from the nineteenth century to today. In the first phase (1880s–1930s), Mexicans were recruited to work on the railroads and do agricultural work in the newly acquired lands of the Southwest (coinciding with the exclusion of Asians). But with the economic challenges of the Great Depression, approximately one million Mexicans were deported. In the second phase (circa 1939), because immigration was closed to the Asiatic Zone when European migration was suspended during World War II, the need for agricultural workers in the West and Southwest once again motivated US companies to employ seasonal workers from Mexico. This was legislated by the US government's *bracero* program (1942–64), that encouraged millions of Mexicans to cross the border, again as guest workers. Yet, eventually, shifting economic fortunes and anti-immigrant sentiment once again restricted movement of Mexicans into the United States. In the most recent phase US economic interests have exploited the ties and geographic proximity by moving production sites to Mexico, while Mexican workers seeking a way out of death-wage economies (created by US exploitation and globalization) continue to cross boundaries and seek opportunities on US soil.

Throughout the twentieth century discrimination against Mexican Americans paralleled that against Black Americans; we might recall that in the racial hierarchy embedded in the FHA

---

[74] Gonzalez, *Harvest of Empire*, 59.

lending manual, Mexicans were last in the hierarchy of racialized lending. This manual was used until at least 1951 and influenced generational access to homeownership. Contemporary discrimination continues to disadvantage Latinos in America.[75] At the same time, Mexican Americans and Mexicans in America were relegated to non-White schools; it was only in 1957 that the segregation of Mexican Americans in public schools was outlawed.[76] Also, like their African American compatriots, Latino Americans often experienced being second-class citizens even in the church.[77]

This history of White supremacy feeding on the bodies and work of those racialized as non-White continues in the United States today with the ongoing debate on immigration and the racial profiling and deporting of non-White persons. And US citizens and policymakers continue to be comfortable with exploitative relationships in American-Mexican trade agreements where US economic growth comes at the expense of our neighbors to the south.

In the racial project of the United States, Latinos have found themselves in a peculiar position. With a dualistic color line of Black and White, state policy identifies Latinos as an ethnic group and requires a choice between this color dualism. In the politics of categorization, Latinos are forced "to place themselves along a sharply drawn color line that separates Blacks and Whites and has remained relatively inflexible over time."[78] In the religio-racial

---

[75] Sanjaya Desliva and Yuval Elmelech, "Housing Inequality in the United States: Explaining the White-Minority Disparities in Homeownership," *Housing Studies* 27, no. 1 (January 2012): 1–26.

[76] Gonzalez, *Harvest of Empire*, 173.

[77] Hector Avalos, *Introduction to the US Latina and Latino Religious Experience* (Boston: Brill, 2004); Virgil Elizondo, "A Report on Racism: A Mexican American in the United States," in *The Church and Racism* (New York: Seabury Press, 1982).

[78] Reanne Frank, Ilana Redstone Akresh, and Bo Lu, "Latino Immigrants and the US Racial Order: How and Where Do They Fit In?" *American Sociological Review* 75, no. 3 (2010): 380, citing F. J. Davis, *Who Is Black: One Nation's Definition* (State College: Pennsylvania State University Press, 1991).

project of America as a White Christian nation, the shifting witchcraft of White supremacy has made room for some at the continued expense of others.

> Historically, many European immigrant groups, including Irish, Jewish and Italian immigrants were originally seen and treated as non-White. Over time, they succeeded in expanding the boundary of Whiteness to include their own ethnic origin groups. Whether Whiteness will expand again to incorporate newer Latino immigrant groups remains an unanswered question.[79]

While the expanding boundary of Whiteness may seem like a salvation in a White Christian nation, it comes at a cost of trading in the currency of White Christian supremacy. By stretching the boundaries of Whiteness, the witchcraft of White supremacy continues.

ANALYZING AMERICA'S RELIGIO-RACIAL PROJECTS: THE WITCHCRAFT OF WHITE SUPREMACY

Despite the differences in the various religio-racial projects, a clear pattern emerges across very different times and places. Again and again White American Christians participated in a society that enacted White supremacy; again and again White Christians participated in attitudes, policies, and actions that were rooted in White supremacy and served to create White superiority. While there were White Christians who resisted these acts of supremacy—Joseph Barndt, for example, charts the resistance when he sees this history as a "tale of two churches," one racist, one anti-racist—it cannot be denied that the dispossession of non-White, non-Christian others in a White Christian nation was the religio-racial project of White Christians. When White Christians used theology to deny land ownership to non-White,

---

[79] Ibid., 381.

non-Christian First Nations, they enjoyed the benefits of land ownership and denied them to their non-White, non-Christian neighbors. When White Christians mobilized Christian identity and Christian theology to deny citizenship to Asians, Whites enjoyed benefits of Asian work as it contributed to the nation but denied the privileges of citizenship to their Asian, non-Christian others. When White Christians enslaved Africans and maintained the system of enslavement over generations, when they later denied full citizenship rights, and barred access to homeownership, Whites laid the foundation of their own well-being while denying them to Black neighbors, mobilizing Christian communities to do so.[80] When White Christians exploit the work of racialized Latino citizens and neighbors, they continue to feed a White Christian nation on the bodies of others. When White theologians say nothing to disrupt this exploitative relationship, their theological production protects White interests. In the words of James Cone, "No group has done more in defining the public meaning of the gospel than White scholars. And no group has done more to corrupt its meaning, making Christianity seem compatible with White supremacy."[81] Through the witchcraft of White supremacy, White Christians created the conditions for their own well-being in one of the richest nations of the globe on the backs and bodies of non-White, non-Christian others.[82]

Recognizing discrimination in land and home ownership, citizenship, and employment is important because of the way each of

---

[80] McGreevy, *Parish Boundaries*.

[81] James Cone, "Black Liberation Theology and Black Catholics: A Critical Conversation," *Theological Studies* 61 (2000): 745.

[82] The culpability of White Christians does not erase the fact that White Christians also joined others in resistance to White Christian supremacy. That each of the legislative arguments had to be mounted reflects the reality that other White Christians resisted this witchcraft (see Barndt, *Becoming an Anti-Racist Church*). However, recognizing that Christians did mount resistance to these supremacist legislations does not discount the fact that it was White Christians who participated in the building up of themselves within a White Christian nation at the dispossession of others.

these functions in the process of wealth accumulation and transmission. When government programs direct resources to White citizens and deny them to Black, Latino, and Native peoples, White citizens benefit generationally. Choices enacted through government programs supported the well-being of Whites through public higher education (Morill Land Grant Act, 1862), the establishment of federal housing assistance and mortgages (FHA, established 1934), social security (established in 1935, but excluding farm workers and domestic workers, professions inhabited largely by African Americans and Latino Americans), and other racially infused legislation. White Christians in America supported choices to keep Black and Brown bodies from White places (*Plessy v. Ferguson,* 1896), White schools (2nd Morill Land Grant Act, 1890), White neighborhoods (FHA Mortgage Underwriting Manual 1934–1951), and White churches. These racialized historic choices form the generational legacy of dispossession that forms the fabric of our society even today. The White family who purchased a home under the racist lending manual in 1934 could then pass on that wealth to the next generation, who could afford to live in a place with good schools, and that again could be passed along to the next generation, so that in 2017 the benefits I enjoy as a White citizen have been passed on to me from a history of racist dispossession. If White Christians participated in the creation of a weighted world in which our Black and Latino neighbors bear more weight on every measure of human well-being, and First Nations peoples are refused the bounty of this land, then the response to the racialized inequalities in our world does not require the response of charity; it requires repentance and reparation.

It was Christians who created the conditions of White supremacy, not merely as a deadly ideology, but now also as a subject position. This is what Perkinson helps us name as the witchcraft of White supremacy: where White Christians made claims about the inferiority of non-White persons and then enacted legislation to create the conditions of their dispossession that would lead to the appearance of White superiority. But what is clear in reviewing this history is that White Christians made choices to *create* the conditions of White supremacy and non-White oppression. White Christians shifted the weight of the world onto their non-White neighbors so that they might enjoy a subject position of superiority. White Christians chose to enslave Black Africans and dispossess First Nations peoples. It was White Christians who established the rules of citizenship and barred any who did not measure up to the standard of "free white persons" of good (Christian) moral standing. White Christians designed a society in which benefits would be shared among citizens, even as these citizens were assessed on the basis of their Whiteness and how close they came to the measures of (White) Christian morality. White Christians invited non-Christian others to build the White Christian nation, and then enacted legislation that said they were not White enough and not Christian enough to share in the benefits of that nation as citizens. White Christians terrorized Black persons and burned Black bodies in the name of this (White) Christian morality. And the undercurrents of (White) Christian morality continue to funnel resources to incarcerate Black and Brown bodies rather than educate Black and Brown minds.[83] White Christians dispossessed First Nations peoples of their lands and continue to argue for the supremacy of European (Christian) nations in the right to those lands.

As guardians of symbolic capital in America's religio-racial project of White Christian supremacy, theologians are not only responsible for the past constructions of ideologies of White supremacy and conditions of dispossession for people of color. Those past constructions of White Christian supremacy created the conditions of the racialized disparity we experience in the United States today. A closer look at the reality of racialized disparity that is our inheritance helps illuminate White supremacy as structural reality and subject position that Christian theology must work to undo.

---

[83] For a comprehensive study of America's racialized incarceration system, see Michelle Alexander, *The New Jim Crow: Mass Incarceration in the Age of Colorblindness* (New York: New Press, 2012).

3

WHEN WORDS
CREATE WORLDS

IN ORDER FOR CHRISTIANS TO respond to present realities of racism and racial disparity, the history of the United States must be narrated in such a way that we see clearly how Christian supremacy gave birth to White supremacy. Furthermore, we need to recognize that a theologically informed ideology of White supremacy created a society structured to prioritize White well-being. By manufacturing the ideology of White Christian supremacy, theologians and thinkers provided the logic for legislation that would dispossess Native peoples, make enslavement seem reasonable, maintain the disenfranchisement of Black citizens, extract the labor of Asian and Latino workers, all the while directing material resources to elevate the subject position of White citizens through land ownership and homeownership, education, health, and security. The generational legacy of this unequal distribution forms the landscape of racialized disparity today.

As our discussion has unearthed, discriminatory practices were woven through America's history with the theological support of White Christian thought. But the Christian vision is not solely one of White well-being. Quite the contrary, strands of the Christian vision propose well-being for all. At the center of Catholic social teaching, as but one example of what Christian tradition calls forth, a vision of human flourishing stands in stark contrast to the history we have recounted. As *Gaudium et Spes* describes:

> There must be made available to all men everything necessary for leading a life truly human, such as food, clothing, and shelter; the right to choose a state of life freely and to found a family; the right to education, to employment, to a good reputation, to respect, to appropriate information, to activity in accord with the upright norm of one's conscience, to protection of privacy, and to rightful freedom in matters religious too. (no. 26)

Note the qualities of a fully human life that the bishops at Vatican II outlined as part of the social vision for our world: food, clothing, shelter, choosing one's state of life, founding a family, and the rights to education, employment, and respect. Through a White racial frame, these benefits in the United States reflect the virtuousness of those who enjoy them, reflecting God's favor and the graces God gives, perhaps even anticipating the eschatological kingdom of God. Yet the long view of America's racial projects shows that these rights were secured for White Christians while systematically denied to others. Such racial projects were supported by theological thinking about God's design reflected in a hierarchy of humanity that informed legislation that dispossessed and disempowered non-White peoples. This history of theological thinking and legislation has had a generational impact that remains with us today. With the initial investment of government support for White well-being, White Americans built up resources and status over time; those denied an initial investment and dispossessed by labor theft and land theft were refused the generational effects of capital accumulation. White supremacy has become embedded in the very structures of US society such that White citizens inhabit prime social locations. If Christians are guided by a vision that desires well-being *for all*, we must see clearly the effects of the sins of the past and the continuing sins of the present that make White supremacy a structural reality.

CONTOURS OF A WEIGHTED WORLD:
MATERIAL REALITIES

To grasp the structural reality of White supremacy as a subject position we might begin with the lens of economic stability. Here, the Pew Research Center starkly reports that in the United States: "In 2013, the most recent year available, the median net worth of households headed by whites was roughly 13 times that of black households ($144,200 for whites compared with $11,200 for blacks)."[1] Latino households also find their economic standing significantly lower than White households, with a median net worth of $13,700.[2] This wealth has been built up generationally in a nation that legislated a priority for White well-being in education, title to land, and homeownership. The generational effect of this economic reality is that although 4.2 million White children in the United States are poor, 4 million Black children and 3.6 million Latino children are also poor, significantly higher percentages of their populations. Poverty, then, is a problem that spans the racial categories of our nation, but on the basic measure of economic stability, people of color collectively have been disadvantaged.

Patterns of both interpersonal and institutionalized racism form the fabric of economic disparity. While interpersonal racism may be familiar to us as discrete acts of discrimination, when these discriminatory actions build up over time and inform social structures they become institutionalized. Disparity is woven through the systems of society and results in,

> differential access to the goods, services, and opportunities of society by race. Institutionalized racism is normative, sometimes legalized, and often manifests as inherited disadvantage. It is structural, having been codified in our

---

[1] Pew Research Center, "On Views of Race and Inequality, Blacks and Whites Are Worlds Apart," 8.

[2] Jens Manuel Krogstad and Antonio Flores, Pew Research Center, "Latinos Made Economic Strides in 2015 after Years of Few Gains."

institutions of custom, practice, and law, so there need not
be an identifiable perpetrator.[3]

The dispossession of Native peoples from their land under-
mined their economic opportunities when land ownership and
the transference of title were reserved for White Christians.
Exclusions from education and fair employment for Black and
Latino populations in our nation's history kept them from economic opportunities that would be transferred generationally.
When generational factors create the conditions for the current
generation of people of color to be economically disadvantaged,
we can name this as the after effects of prior decisions and identify it as institutionalized racism. But interpersonal racism has
not disappeared from the scene. Sociologists report that African
Americans continue to be "discriminated against in the labor
market, concentrated in blue collar employment, and, along with
Latinos, particularly dark skinned Latinos like Puerto Ricans,
earn the lowest wages."[4] Economic disparity demonstrates the
structural effects of institutional racism and the ongoing impact
of interpersonal racism.

Among the key institutional factors that inform dramatic economic disparity is homeownership, which offers a stark portrait
of a world where some have security in an owned home and
others do not. Homeownership disproportionately favors White
Americans; the US Census Bureau reports that 72 percent of
White Americans own homes, while only 45 percent of Latino

---

[3] Camara Phyllis Jones, "Levels of Racism: A Theoretic Framework
and a Gardener's Tale," *American Journal of Public Health* (August
2000): 1212.

[4] Meghan Kuebler and Jacob Rugh, "New Evidence on Racial and
Economic Disparities in Homeownership in the United States from 2001
to 2010," *Social Science Research* 42 (2013): 1371. See also M. Anne
Visser and Edwin Meléndez, "Puerto Ricans in the US Low-Wage Labor
Market: Introduction to the Issues, Trends, and Policies," *CENTRO
Journal* 23, no. 11 (Fall 2011): 5, which states: "Research has shown that
Puerto Ricans are concentrated in low-wage jobs and experience higher
rates of unemployment and poverty than other Hispanic subgroups."

Americans and 41 percent of Black Americans do. Homeowner-ship is the most important source of building wealth and transfer-ring it generationally.[5] Through government-sponsored programs that benefit homeowners and tax codes that support them, leg-islation and policy provide economic benefit to those who own homes. Further, the equity that homeowners accrue has been a significant feature of borrowing capacity as well as a source of income that homeowners access in cases when the property is sold at a profit. But when the government helped White families purchase homes, and then White families profited when property values rose, the initial investment made with government help ultimately supported the economic well-being of Whites. Profit from increased property value can translate into money avail-able for investing, higher education, and other forms of benefit that are passed on in family systems. When Black and Latino families were barred from purchasing homes, they could not benefit from the initial government investment and generational wealth accumulation. Even today, when poor families pay more than half their income in rent and are not accumulating the long-term benefits of equity, their generational buildup of economic capital is compromised. The housing disparity, then, is the result of economic disparity, but it also stems from the actively racist patterns in our nation's history of prioritizing housing for White citizens and employing a racial hierarchy in mortgage lending that placed Black and Latino citizens in last place for obtaining mortgages. When White Christian congregations mobilized to restrict African Americans and Latinos from purchasing homes

---

[5] Sanjaya Desliva and Yuval Elmelech, "Housing Inequality in the United States: Explaining the White-Minority Disparities in Homeown-ership," *Housing Studies* 27, no. 1 (January 2012): 2. See also R. Fry, R. Kochhar, and P. Taylor, "Wealth Gaps Rise to Record Highs between Whites, Blacks, Hispanics: Twenty-to-One," Pew Research Center (July 26, 2011): "A sizeable minority of US households own no assets other than a motor vehicle. In 2009, that was true for 24 percent of black and Hispanic households, 8 percent of Asian households and 6 percent of white households."

in their neighborhoods, they made decisions that would build up White Christians at the expense of non-White, non-Christian others. Today's disparity also results from more recent patterns of targeting communities of color with predatory lending that has taken place in the years from 2001 to 2010.[6] As Sanjaya Desliva and Yuval Elmelech report, summarizing the work of others:

> Disparities in homeownership have been conceived primarily as reverberations of differences in wealth generated by forces such as slavery, sharecropping, and redlining that echoed, however powerfully, from a distant past. Although past mechanisms that perpetuated stratification by place and race may have been vanquished under the law, new forms of discrimination may have arisen. One such recent institutional barrier to minority homeownership is reverse redlining. A pattern of unfair provision of high cost or subprime loans on the basis of race and neighborhood racial composition, reverse redlining and its implications have been documented and explored by a growing body of research. The dramatic rise of subprime lending introduced a contemporary mechanism that reified racial disparities in homeownership.[7]

The sins of the past in prioritizing White well-being created the sinful condition of racialized disparity in homeownership and interpersonal racism that persists in this field.

Homeownership remains important not only as entry to generational wealth accumulation but also as the door through which people access other sources of human well-being. As Alex Mikulich reminds us, "Owning a home and housing location are

---

[6] Meghan Kuebler and Jacob Rugh, "New Evidence on Racial and Economic Disparities in Homeownership in the United States from 2001 to 2010," *Social Science Research* 42 (2013): 1359. See also Gregory D. Squires, "Predatory Lending: Redlining in Reverse," *Shelterforce Online* (National Housing Institute) (January/February 2005).

[7] Desliva and Elmelech, "Housing Inequality in the United States, 1–26.

critical to predicting access to quality education, development
of personal wealth, employment, health and safety, democratic
participation, transportation and quality child care."[8] In addition
to generational transference of wealth through homeownership,
access to education intertwines with this racialized financial disparity. Funding for primary and secondary schools in the United
States draws first and foremost on local property taxes. While
the federal government supplies our schools with approximately
12 percent of their budget, and state funds contribute another
44 percent, the remaining 44 percent of funding for education
is derived from local government. The heavy reliance on local
taxes connects educational opportunities with homeownership
and wealth. According to the New America Foundation website:

> Property taxes support most of the funding that local
> government provides for education. Local governments
> collect taxes from residential and commercial properties
> as a direct revenue source for the local school district.
> Wealthier, property-rich localities have the ability to collect
> more in property taxes. Having more resources to draw
> from enables the district to keep tax rates low while still
> providing adequate funding to their local school districts.
> Poorer communities with less of a property tax base may
> have higher tax rates, but still raise less funding to support
> the local school district. This can often mean that children
> that live in low-income communities with the highest needs
> go to schools with the least resources, the least qualified
> teachers, and substandard school facilities.

In 2010, Linda Darling-Hammond reported that wealthy suburbs
spend twice as much as cities on education and three times as

---

[8] Alex Mikulich and Jeannine Hill Fletcher, "Racial Equity Practices
at the Service of the Magis," plenary session for the Mission Matters:
Moving from Strong Words to Courageous Actions conference spon-
sored by the Association of Jesuit Colleges and Universities, Conference
on Diversity and Equity, Santa Clara University, Santa Clara, California,
June 20, 2016.

much as poor rural areas.[9] An earlier study reports, "At the national level, schools with a majority of students of color are 3.7 times more likely to be severely overcrowded than schools with less than 5 percent students of color."[10] In addition to disparities between low-income and high-income school districts researchers note disparities within school districts, related to the allocation of teachers. "Higher-paid, more experienced teachers tend to be congregated in lower-needs schools, while less-experienced teachers end up in high-needs schools."[11] Schools with a higher-income parent base may also see private support of the schools in fundraising, PTA involvement, and other resources made available when families have money, time, and expertise. Access to wealth translates to access to homeownership in a high-income neighborhood, which translates to access to a well-funded educational system, and we begin to see the interlocking systems by which America's children of color are disproportionately educated in under-resourced schools.

When homeownership and median wealth show evidence of disparity along race lines, and primary and secondary education are directly tied to homeownership and wealth, it is unsurprising that access to higher education, too, reflects racialized inequalities. The National Center for Education Statistics reported that in 2009–10 degrees ranging from associate's through doctorates were largely conferred on White students.[12] The US Census Bu-

---

[9] Linda Darling-Hammond, "Restoring Our Schools," *The Nation*, May 27, 2010.

[10] Race Forward: The Center for Racial Justice Innovation, "Report Charges Racial Profiling in US Public Schools," *Race Forward: The Center for Racial Justice Innovation* (April 13, 2006).

[11] "School Finance," New America EdCentral (Washington, DC).

[12] National Center for Education Statistics, *Digest of Education Statistics: 2015*, https://nces.ed.gov/programs/digest/d15/. Data from this report indicates: "Between 2003–04 and 2013–14, the number of White students earning bachelor's degrees increased 19 percent, compared with larger increases of 46 percent for Black students, 114 percent for Hispanic students. . . . In 2013–14, White students earned 68 percent of all bachelor's degrees awarded (vs. 76 percent in 2003–04), Black students earned 11 percent (vs. 10 percent in 2003–04), Hispanic students earned 11 percent (vs. 7 percent in 2003–04)."

reau reports that 29 percent of Whites in the United States (twenty-five years of age or older) hold a degree from a four-year college, while 17 percent of Black and 13 percent of Latinos do; this builds on an 80 percent high school graduation rate for Whites, 62 percent for Blacks, 68 percent for Latinos, and 51 percent for Native Americans.[13] Access to a college education that will enhance a person's chances for economic security in the future is dependent upon what one had access to in the past. If a quality primary and secondary school education is disproportionately withheld from Black and Latino students as a result of an education system built upon property taxes and wealth held in communities (and not shared beyond local districts), this shaky foundation will yield fewer Black and Latino students prepared for college. Current trends that reverse the important decisions of desegregation in 1954 should be an alarming pattern, but it is not clear that the alarm has been sounded to raise Americans' concern.[14]

Given the high cost of higher education, even highly qualified students of color are not accessing the most prestigious colleges and universities at the same rate as their White counterparts. A 2013 report from Georgetown University's Center for Education and the Workforce described the landscape of higher education as "separate and unequal," showing data that indicates that White students disproportionately fill seats in elite colleges and universities, while Black and Latino students—equally qualified—are finding their education at public colleges and universities.[15] The report's executive summary states their findings:

---

[13] Stella U. Ogunwole, Malcolm Drewery, Jr., and Merarys Rios-Vargas, "The Population with a Bachelor's Degree or Higher by Race and Hispanic Origin: 2006–2010" (Washington, DC: US Census Bureau, May 2012).

[14] "Brown at 60: Great Progress, a Long Retreat, and an Uncertain Future," The Civil Rights Project (UCLA) (May 2014).

[15] Anthony Carneval and Jeff Strohl, "Separate and Unequal: How Higher Education Reinforces the Intergenerational Reproduction of White Racial Privilege," Georgetown Center on Education and the Workforce (July 2013).

Between 1995 and 2009, 82 percent of new white freshman enrollments were at the 468 most selective four-year colleges, compared to 13 percent for Hispanics and 9 percent for African-Americans; 68 percent of new African American freshman enrollments and 72 percent of new Hispanic freshman enrollments were at open-access two-year and four-year colleges, compared to no growth for whites.[16]

Disparity and segregation in our residential communities are translating to disparities and segregation in our institutions of education.

The Pew report "Twenty-to-One" provides a lens on our world that shows how disparity in wealth is inextricably linked to other sites of disparity, with homeownership and education being key among them. These systems of our society support the accumulation of economic capital, as well as what sociologists describe as "human capital"—those benefits that accrue to persons as the result of education, social standing, experience, and so on.[17] Human capital rests on the foundation of personal health. When health measures like diabetes, obesity, heart disease, and infant mortality also favor White Americans, we must see that systems for well-being disproportionately fail Americans of color.[18]

---

[16] Ibid.

[17] See, for example, the use of the concept of human capital in William Vélez and Giovanni Burgos, "The Impact of Housing Segregation and Structural Factors on the Socioeconomic Performance of Puerto Ricans in the United States," *CENTRO Journal* 23, no. 1 (Spring 2010): 174–97.

[18] The US Department of Health and Human Services reports the following diabetes rates: 6.2 percent Whites; 10.8 percent Blacks; 10.6 percent Latino; 9.0 percent Native American. The Centers for Disease Control reports the infant mortality rates per 1,000 live births: 6/1,000 Whites; 12/1,000 Blacks, 6/1,000 Latino, 8/1,000 Native American. A study using similar measures in Canada found that the health disparities of White and Black Canadians did not always favor Whites, attributing health outcomes to the more recent immigration of Black Canadians to North America and the long-term negative status of Black Americans and the legacy of slavery and the structural dispossession after slavery

Although disproportionately in need of healthcare, the National Academy of Science also records disparity in the quality of health care that runs along racial lines. Opening their study bluntly, their findings report that "racial and ethnic minorities tend to receive a lower quality of healthcare than non-minorities, even when access-related factors, such as patients' insurance status and income are controlled."[19] Those who are seen as non-White experience interpersonal discrimination but are also the recipients of generational exclusions, all of which collectively influence health outcomes that vary by race. But, as epidemiologist and healthcare expert Camara Phyllis Jones indicates from her work on racial disparity in health outcomes, "the variable 'race' is not a biological construct that reflects innate differences, but a social construct that precisely captures the impacts of racism."[20] Denied equal access to health through structural and interpersonal vehicles, the bodily integrity of non-White persons is also compromised by taking employment in systems that exchange workers' well-being for the health of the nation. For example, in the food system that supports the overall health of Americans, migrant Latino farmworkers are statistically "more likely than any other ethnic group to be involved in a fatal occupational injury."[21] Health and human capital are too often still disproportionately acquired by White Americans to the detriment of people of color.

---

ended. See Lydia Lebrun and Thomas A. LaVeist, "Black/White Racial Disparities in Health: A Cross-Country Comparison of Canada and the United States" Research Letter, *Journal of Internal Medicine* 171, no. 17 (September 26, 2011). Among Puerto Ricans who participated in an NIH study of Latino health, 36 percent reported having asthma, 20 percent diabetes, 46 percent obesity (see National Institute of Health, "Hispanic Community Health Study (HCHS)/Study of Latinos (SOL)."

[19] Brian D. Smedley, Adrienne Y. Stith, and Alan R. Nelson, eds., Committee on Understanding and Eliminating Racial and Ethnic Disparities in Health Care, *Unequal Treatment: Confronting Racial and Ethnic Disparities in Health Care* (Washington, DC: National Academies Press, 2003).

[20] Jones, "Levels of Racism, 1212.

[21] MCN (Migrant Clinicians Network), "The Migrant/Seasonal Farmworker."

Just as bodily integrity in health disproportionately favors White Americans, bodily security demonstrates the effects of racism in the United States. When incarceration rates for Black and Latino Americans are disproportionate to the adult population, structural disparities of policing and security indicate that our social practices support the struggle for White well-being in ways that shift the weight of the world onto Blacks and Latinos.[22]

STRUCTURAL WHITE SUPREMACY AS A KINGDOM OF EVIL

The White racial frame looks out on the world and sees God's favor blessing people with well-being; through God's grace and White virtuousness, White Americans enjoy bodily well-being, security, health, education, green space, homeownership, and economic security. A kingdom of God would extend these benefits of well-being to all people. But when a White racial frame looks upon our world and sees the distribution of benefits affirming White virtuousness, while ignoring White Christian dispossession of non-White, non-Christian peoples, it willfully ignores the ways in which White well-being has been created. In Feagin's view the White racial frame rests fundamentally on the classification of human beings, where White people and Whiteness are viewed positively and virtuously (ignoring the history of White decimation and exploitation of people of color), while the racial other is

---

[22] Michelle Alexander, *The New Jim Crow: Mass Incarceration in the Age of Colorblindness*, rev. ed. (New York: The New Press, 2012). Alexander charts the way that racialized application of drug laws in the United States have led to the policing of non-White communities and the incarceration of non-White persons radically different from the policing and incarceration of White communities and persons. Centering in on drug laws that have disproportionately jailed Black and Latino men, Alexander writes, "The war on drugs could have been waged primarily in overwhelmingly white suburbs or on college campuses" (124). But it was not.

constructed as less virtuous or "unvirtuous."[23] In the unconscious deep logic of the White racial frame, White people are judged to be more intelligent and hard working, with an entitlement to what they have in economic security, education, and bodily health (ignoring the history of federal assistance programs that provided these benefits unequally for Whites).[24] The foundation of the White racial frame assesses people of color while ignoring the history of "unjust enrichment and unjust impoverishment" designed with the well-being of White people in view.[25]

If we are able to displace the White racial frame as the interpretive lens for our field of vision, we might see in the current racialized disparity not a foretaste of the kingdom of God, but the reality of a kingdom of evil. People of color in the United States are systematically denied well-being in economic capital, bodily security, health, recreation, education, and ownership. Americans have come to accept this structural reality as part of the order of things, normalizing dispossession, placing it in the past, and ignoring its generational effects. But a world that is saturated and structured by White supremacy can only be described as a kingdom of evil. In the words of Walter Rauschenbusch, "The life of humanity is infinitely interwoven, always renewing itself, yet always perpetuating what has been. The evils of one generation are caused by the wrongs of generations that preceded, and will in turn condition the sufferings and temptations of those who

---

[23] Joe R. Feagin, *The White Racial Frame: Centuries of Racial Framing and Counter-Framing* (New York: Routledge, 2010), 96.

[24] Federal assistance programs dedicated to the well-being of Whites include, but are not limited to, Citizenship (1790); Homestead Act (1862); Land-Grant universities (1862); Federal Housing Administration (1934); Social Security (1934), which did not include agricultural workers and domestic workers (occupations dominated by African American and Latino workers); transportation funding that brought highways to White suburbs (1950s); and "slum clearance" that disrupted many communities of color (1970s).

[25] Feagin, *The White Racial Frame*, 96.

come after."[26] As Christian theologians strive after the kingdom of God, we need to name our current realities of racialized disparity as a kingdom of evil that past systems have created and the current status quo maintains.

To think our way out of the kingdom of evil, which racial disparity represents and reflects, we might theorize about our human condition with the help of theologian and critical theorist Mark Lewis Taylor. Taylor probes beneath the surface of our everyday lives to imagine who we are as humans at the level of being or ontology.[27] Taylor's is a social ontology, which means that the very basis of who we are is not found as individuals but is found only as individuals emerge from and are situated within the collective, the social. Taylor proposes that human beings are irreducibly enmeshed in relations and locations that shape who we are, how we feel, and what our bodies have access to. He asks us to imagine our social existence at its most basic level as holding the possibility that we might exist in "a delicate spacing of bodies, involving both mutual intimacy and distancing of bodies."[28] We are as human beings situated within the social, and there is the possibility for *all* to thrive in our fundamental relatedness. Embedded in networks of relationship to others, we strive for our personal well-being, but this does not necessitate compromising the well-being of others. Taylor envisions that we could be constituted by bodies in balance where we struggle together for our shared well-being. In this ideal case we would share the weight of the world using our individual power to maintain the well-being not only of ourselves but of the collective.

While this potential power equilibrium *should* ontologically, and *could* theoretically, frame our existence as human beings,

---

[26] Walter Rauschenbusch, *A Theology for the Social Gospel (1917)* (Louisville, KY: Westminster John Knox Press, 1997), 79.

[27] Mark Lewis Taylor, *The Theological and the Political: On the Weight of the World* (Minneapolis: Fortress Press, 2011).

[28] Ibid., 41.

our world is constituted instead by a tragic history in which the
weight of the world is shifted onto some and lifted from others.[29]
This disequilibrium is maintained by the constant exertion of
power where some struggle to maintain the weightlessness that
is experienced when weight is lifted from them and shifted onto
others. Taylor's anthropology characterizes all human beings in
the push and pull of a constant struggle: the privileged struggle
to maintain their position and well-being, while the dispossessed
struggle to achieve well-being. He uses the term *agonistic* to describe the struggle and sees it as political.

Our enmeshment within the agonistic political is structured
not only by human relationships of sharing material resources
but also through the symbolic capital that names the persons and
things with which we share our space. As humans struggle for
bodily securities (capital in both economic and material senses),
we also struggle for recognition, which comes from the reservoir
of symbolic capital. As Taylor describes it, "There is . . . both an
egoistic pursuit of self-love and a fascination with, and need to
secure, approval of others. Glory, honor, credit, praise, fame—
these make up the currency of symbolic capital."[30]

With the struggle for survival and the struggle to secure
approval, Taylor provides a theory to explain the history of
dispossession and structural inequality. Simply put, when White
Christians struggled to secure their well-being, they shifted the
weight of the world onto non-White, non-Christian others. It
is within the disequilibrium of a weighted world that people
continue to struggle for recognition and well-being. We live in
a "weighted world," where the dispossessed bear more while
the privileged bear less, yet both struggle to achieve recognition
through material and symbolic capital. Instead of a world where
bodies are in balance and persons enjoy both place and meaning in the world, our world is out of balance. Some among us

---

[29] Ibid. Taylor references Ian James, *The Fragmentary Demand: An
Introduction to the Philosophy of Jean-Luc Nancy* (Stanford, CA: Stanford University Press, 2006), 79.

[30] Taylor, *The Theological and the Political,* 88.

are prized, and others devalued; some have material well-being, and others do not.

The disequilibrium is evident in the material conditions of unequal capital, and it is fueled by systems of symbolic capital that recognize and name some bodies as worthy and others as not. Because the world is figured both materially (as bodies sharing space) and linguistically (as bodies embedded in meaning), we can see that persons move through the world in a way that is informed not only by bodily needs but also by meaning conferred on them. While the conferral of symbolic capital allows persons to be recognized as valuable within the world—they are recognized as having worth and are welcomed members of a meaningful world—Taylor notes patterns of dispossession on which sociality has been structured. Through value-laden oppositions, some bodies are rendered less than others. This means that some persons experience "misrecognition"; they are cast out of the web of sociality or relegated to its underside. This tragic reality of misrecognition and dispossession compromises the delicate equilibrium of bodies in balance. More tragically, this disequilibrium is not challenged when guardians of symbolic capital manufacture meanings that allow this devaluation to be normalized. In Taylor's words, "The oppositions are made to seem—and not just cognitively, but in social actors' reflexive and spontaneous understandings—'natural,' part of the order of things."[31] In a weighted world, the "natural" dispossession of the misrecognized is counterpart to the conferral of symbolic capital by which *only some* receive "glory, honor, credit, praise, fame."[32] The value-laden oppositions created and conferred by symbolic capital provide a logical hierarchy of greater and lesser worth that is translated into hierarchies of fair and unfair treatment. This creates the condition where some persons in our world are not recognized as worthy and experience instead the shifting of weight onto them.[33] It is the guardians of symbolic capital

---

[31] Ibid., 90–91.
[32] Ibid., 88.
[33] Ibid., 89.

who inform and maintain the world's meanings and practices in a matrix of sociality, and the conferral of meaning produces a security of material benefits as well.

The root conception of what is more valuable and its continued structuring form what appears as "part of the order of things."[34] Reading this normalization of unequal balance through the history of homeownership, education, and economic security, the weighted world of the United States has allowed racialized dispossession to appear normal. Racial disparity was legalized in the systems by which White Americans came to homeownership at a rate of 70 percent and Black Americans only at a rate of 47 percent and Latino Americans at a rate of 46 percent. In the United States, we've normalized the reality that Black and Latino youth will be found in greater number in the under-resourced and failing schools. In the United States, we've normalized the reality that there are nearly the same number of Black children and White children living in poverty, although White children constitute three times more of the population than Black children do. We've implicitly said it's acceptable for higher percentages of people of color to be poor and experience hunger and premature death just because "that's the way things are."[35] On the many criteria for "a life fully human" as articulated by *Gaudium et Spes*, poverty compromises human flourishing in an interconnected web of housing, security, food, education, respect, privacy, and more.

The concern for our weighted world ought to be the concern of Christians, not only because it compromises the humanity of our neighbors, but because Christian ideology and Christian theology played a key role in creating the weighted world. The disposses-

---

[34] Ibid., 90–91.

[35] Poverty rates from 2007–11: US population as a whole, 14.3 percent; Blacks, 25.8 percent; Native Americans, 27 percent; Hispanics, 23.2 percent; Asians, 11.7 percent; Whites, 11.6 percent (Suzanne Macartney, Alemayehu Bishaw, and Kayla Fontenot, "Poverty Rates for Selected Detailed Race and Hispanic Groups by State and Place: 2007–2011" (February 2013), http//www.census.gov/prod/2013pubs/acsbr11–17.pdf).

sion of Native peoples rested on dishonoring and discrediting their character and their culture. The dehumanization and deliberate rejection of Black Americans aligned with assigning honor and praise to Whites. Latino Americans too often found themselves not receiving credit for the work they had done. As we have seen in the preceding chapters, all of this was done with a theo-logic of White Christian supremacy. The symbolic capital of Christian theology created the material disparity of our weighted world.

Camara Phyllis Jones offers an allegoric tale that might help us to imagine the relationship between material capital and symbolic capital in the generational struggle of our weighted world. Her story begins with a gardener who has a preference for red flowers. The gardener also had flower boxes filled with good soil and rocky soil. Jones paints the scene:

> This gardener has 2 packets of seeds for the same type of flower. However, the plants grown from one packet of seeds will bear pink blossoms, while the plants grown from the other packet of seeds will bear red blossoms. The gardener prefers red over pink, so she plants the red seed in the rich fertile soil and the pink seed in the poor rocky soil. . . . All of the red flowers grow up and flourish, with the fittest growing tall and strong and even the weakest making it to a middling height. But in the box with the poor rocky soil, things look different. The weak among the pink seeds don't even make it, and the strongest among them grow only to a middling height.
>
> In time the flowers in these 2 boxes go to seed, dropping their progeny into the same soil in which they were growing. The next year the same thing happens, with the red flowers in the rich soil growing full and vigorous and strong, while the pink flowers in the poor soil struggle to survive. And these flowers go to seed. Year after year, the same thing happens. Ten years later the gardener comes to survey her garden. Gazing at the 2 boxes, she says, "I was right to prefer red over pink! Look how vibrant and

beautiful the red flowers look, and see how pitiful and scrawny the pink ones are."[36]

Jones unpacks this story with a theoretic framework of three levels of racism relevant to our discussion. The gardener has *internalized ideologies* of inferiority and superiority, which come to be expressed in a way that is *personally mediated* through the choice of providing her preferred flower with the resources to grow vibrant and beautiful while providing only poor soil for the unfavored pink flowers where they struggle to survive. The gardener's personal choices inform the *structures* of flourishing in the form of flower boxes of rich or poor soil.

Translating the metaphor to the racial project of privilege and dispossession in the United States, we transpose the framework to ask where *internalized ideologies of racial superiority and inferiority* informed choices of *personally mediated racism,* which created the conditions that are inherited dispossession of *structural or institutionalized racism*. Here, unpacking the root forms of institutionalized racism might help us then turn to apply new insights to theology. One is that of *personally mediated racism*. According to Jones, "*Personally mediated racism* is defined as prejudice and discrimination, where prejudice means differential assumptions about the abilities, motives, and intentions of others according to their race, and discrimination means differential actions toward others according to their race."[37] When the gardener made choices that privileged one flower over the other, she enacted differential actions according to color, mobilizing the value-laden opposition of red versus pink. But personally mediated racism stems from a deeper root cause in *internalized racism*. In the gardener's case the internalized racism of racial superiority creates the conditions for her differential actions. In another episode of this gardener's tale the flowers themselves come to internalize messages of inferiority, leading Jones to name *internalized racism* "as acceptance by members of the stigmatized

---

[36] Jones, "Levels of Racism," 1213.
[37] Ibid., 1212–13.

races of negative messages about their own abilities and intrinsic worth."[38] Internalized racism allows both sides of the value-laden opposition to accept "the order of things" with internal stories about both racial inferiority and racial superiority.[39]

In using Jones's metaphor to probe deeper into the problem of Christian theology supporting White supremacy we might ask where the "gardener" learned the stories of internalized racial superiority and internalized racial inferiority. In generations past she might have learned these stories from the professors and preachers who painted a picture of God's design and human destiny reflected in skin and status. In more recent generations she might hear these stories with the subtle clues that elevate Christian identity, White culture, and its Eurocentric elements. Jones's metaphorical proposal invites us to consider how theology might work at the level of changing ideologies. With the analysis of history and clear sightedness about the reality of racialized disparity, Christian theologians could be mobilizing our stories to change the White racial frame. If a religio-racial project of White Christian supremacy has created the conditions for the racialized disparity we see today, couldn't Christian theologians mobilize their symbolic capital in a *new* religio-racial project, one that recreates our world toward racial justice?

RETRODUCTIVE WARRANT FOR DESK MURDERERS

What we produce in the symbolic capital of our theologies cannot be disentangled from the social and political worlds in which we live. As we saw in Chapters 1 and 2, the building of a White Christian nation was underwritten by theologies of White Christian supremacy. Theologians and thinkers manufactured

---

[38] Ibid., 1213.

[39] While Jones focuses on internalized racial inferiority, the Peoples' Institute for Survival and Beyond antiracist training, Undoing Racism, insists on naming the twin aspects of internalized inferiority and internalized superiority and essential features of internalized racial oppression (http://www.pisab.org).

ideas that counted as knowledge about the hierarchy of humanity, God's design for White well-being, and the inferiority of
non-White, non-Christian others. These ideas produced in the
realm of symbolic capital had the power to influence national
ideology and legislation that channeled resources to White Christians in the form of title to land, access to education, support
for homeownership, and more. All the while, theological ideas
underwrote White supremacy for the dispossession, exploitation,
and generational disadvantage of people of color. Today, Christians
are either culpable in the patterns of White Christian supremacy or
they are actively resistant in producing antiracist, anti-supremacist
theologies. Just as our forebears participated in the religio-racial
project that surrounded the establishment of America as a White
Christian nation, so too our theological production informs the
attitudes and the religio-racial projects of our times.

Recall that for Mark Lewis Taylor *world* is both embodied
(the physical reality in which we are embedded) and conceptual
(the stretch of our vision of meaningfulness). The importance of
world is that our lives as human beings are not primarily individual, but that our being as humans is fundamentally social—
both in terms of the physicality of sharing space with others in
our world, and also in terms of being affected by the sociality of
shared meaning. Meaning and materiality coalesce in the bodies
that inhabit our world. It is meaning that confers justification for
the rights and privileges enjoyed by those who inhabit a world.

As we have seen, instead of a world in balance, where all persons enjoy both bodily well-being and the affirmation that we
belong in this world, our world is out of balance. Some among
us are prized and others devalued. Following the work of soci-
ologist Pierre Bourdieu, Taylor traces the imbalance of worlds
to the production of symbolic capital grounded in "value-laden
opposition." He describes how "oppositions are set up, which
not only organize communal life at [specific] sites, but also link
that communal life to nature and cosmos, thus endowing aspects
of social structure with different meanings and value."[40] When

---

[40] Taylor, *The Theological and the Political*, 90.

worlds are built on the basic structure of opposition, where some are recognized and others erased, those recognized bodies enjoy material benefits that their others do not, and those who are misrecognized are very easily erased.[41] Value-laden oppositions function crucially to normalize an unequal balance and feed the project of misrecognition. The root conception of what is more valuable and its continued structuring form "the order of things."[42] But this imaginative "order of things" doesn't drop from the sky; it is formulated and fostered by those with the time, resources, and symbolic capital to effect wider public sentiment and to confer meaning on some while withholding it from others. We have seen this in our preceding examples, where pastors, politicians, and educators inform religio-racial projects by shaping the symbolic web of meaningfulness, arranging so that some receive "glory, honor, credit, praise, fame"[43] while others are misrecognized—cast out of the web of sociality or relegated to its underside.

In looking to the past we can see the persistent pattern of a theo-logic that rests on the value-laden opposition of Christian versus non-Christian. This value-laden opposition laid the groundwork for the elevated status of Whiteness in the past, but it also continues to function in the America of the present, threatening misrecognition of our religious others. When we can see that theological production in the past has created the conditions for White well-being at the expense of others, and that theologies of supremacy continue to hold significant harm for our neighbors of other faiths, the value of our Christian theological claims must be interrogated with respect to what Francis Schüssler Fiorenza terms the "retroductive warrant" in our theological production. In Schüssler Fiorenza's description, theology unfolds at the dynamic intersection between received inheritance of scripture and tradition, informed by contemporary background theories and engaged with a variety of communities of discourse. Given the

---

[41] Ibid.
[42] Ibid., 90–91.
[43] Ibid., 88.

vast diversity that can be produced by this dynamic mix and shifting set of influences, he suggests that we include also as an element in our theological method the work of the retroductive warrant. He writes:

> A retroductive warrant within the philosophy of science refers to the fertility of a hypothesis, idea or theory. . . . This theoretical and practical fruitfulness is both prospective and retrospective. . . . Theological theory advances not simply by implication or correlation, but rather through the creative suggestion by which the experience of the community's past, present and future is illuminated.[44]

The idea of a retroductive warrant is that Christian interpretations of scripture and tradition must include a weighing of their productive fruitfulness. Employing a retroductive warrant asks us to think about the various networks of thought and material practice within which our theological thinking is situated. Christian theologies emerge from engagement with the biblical texts in light of contemporary theories in a variety of communities of discourse. But this engagement and the theologies thus produced also have material outcomes. The function of a retroductive warrant is to anticipate the material outcomes of our theological thinking. In constructing a contemporary Christian theology, Christians must ask what are the possible outcomes of particular ways of thinking and must be guided practically by the negative outcomes (as well as the positive) that might be anticipated.

The function of a retroductive warrant is not new to twenty-first-century Christians. In hindsight, Christian theologians have

---

[44] Francis Schüssler Fiorenza, "Systematic Theology: Task and Methods," in *Systematic Theology: Roman Catholic Perspectives*, 2nd ed., ed. Francis Schüssler Fiorenza and John Galvin (Minneapolis: Fortress Press, 2011), 58–59. For more on Fiorenza's use of the retroductive warrant, see Terrence Bateman, *Reconstructing Theology: The Contribution of Francis Schüssler Fiorenza* (Minneapolis: Fortress Press, 2014).

taken responsibility for the death-dealing outcomes of Christian supremacist notions directed at the Jews. As Susannah Heschel has shown, the widespread theological production of Christian anti-Semitism that circulated throughout the academic world and into pulpits and political spheres can be traced back to scholars producing symbolic capital in the form of research and "knowledge." Heschel powerfully names these producers in the system as "desk murderers."[45] But, the production of anti-Semitism in the generations prior to the Holocaust was not just the responsibility of the few powerful thinkers who are at the center of Heschel's study. A much broader range of Christian theologians participated in mainstream Christian theology that placed blame on the Jews for the death of Christ. Recognizing their culpability in the outcome of these patterns of thought, post-Holocaust Christian theologians have assumed responsibility for theological claims that might have as their outcome anti-Semitism and the violent trajectory of genocide that was witnessed.[46]

Today, Christians have in the well-being of our neighbors of color and our neighbors of other faiths a practical outcome in view for rethinking Christian claims to superiority and to universality. If we can see how our theologies function in the social matrix of recognition and misrecognition, situated as they are within a weighted world, Christians must forecast the outcomes of their symbolic rendering of our racial and religious others and the interpretation of the Christian story and symbols. Will our theologies leave undisturbed the unjust status quo of White supremacy? Through a White racial frame, will our theologies continue to defend White virtuousness? Will our theologies situate our Muslim, Jewish, and Hindu neighbors as less than fully human, less worthy of recognition? Do our theologies of religions rely upon the hierarchical opposition of Christian/non-Christian such that our symbolic capital is conferred on Christians and

---

[45] Susannah Heschel, *The Aryan Jesus: Christian Theologians and the Bible in Nazi Germany* (Princeton, NJ: Princeton University Press, 2008).

[46] Schüssler Fiorenza, "Systematic Theology," 60.

withheld from others? Or can we formulate theologies that mobilize our symbolic capital for the creation of a different world? Recognizing the sins of the past and the sins of the present that stand at the intersection of White supremacy and Christian superiority, White Christians are asked to create a new theo-logic that seeks the well-being of Black and Brown bodies as well as the well-being of our neighbors of diverse faiths.

Social-science evidence indicates that the gulf between White and Black well-being, as it is grounded in economic resources, remains astounding and that closing the gap remains a distant reality. A 2008 study offered the following projection: "If the racial wealth divide continues to close as slowly as it has since 1983, it will take 634 years for Blacks to reach wealth equality with whites."[47] Economically dispossessed and educationally under-resourced citizens of color continue to disproportionately fill our jails and meet early deaths through policing practices, poverty, and health discriminations; meanwhile, White citizens enjoy superior opportunities in health, homeownership, education, and economic stability. In a White Christian nation people of color who are part of the faith traditions of the globe routinely experience Islamophobia, discrimination, and death-dealing attitudes of Christian supremacy. Knowing that as a theologian I am rich in the currency of symbolic capital, but knowing also how my predecessors have employed the symbolic capital of Christian tradition to contribute to a racial project of White Christian supremacy, I want to return to the storehouse of my tradition to see what new stories we might tell to shape new worlds. What resources might be found in the stories of Christian theology that might be mobilized for a religio-racial project that is the flourishing of all in a multi-religious, multi-racial nation?

---

[47] Dedrick Muhammad, *Forty Years Later: The Unrealized American Dream* (Washington, DC: Institute for Policy Studies, 2008), 5.

4

THE SYMBOLIC CAPITAL
OF NEW TESTAMENT LOVE

THE STORY OF HOW CHRISTIAN supremacy gave birth to White supremacy and, in turn, created the conditions of racialized disparity is the story of White Christians invested in the material conditions of the world such that the ideology they produced and promoted served their needs and secured their personal well-being. The White racial frame reads the unjust distribution of well-being as evidence of White righteousness, rather than recognizing the kingdom of evil that disparity represents. Even if Christians today are not directly responsible for creating the conditions of dispossession and disparity, when we do nothing to change current conditions, the story of our faith and our symbolic capital supports an unjust status quo by default. And yet, we do have the resources to mobilize a rebalancing of the world. They lie deep in the wisdom of our tradition as we might tell the story of Jesus in new ways. In the light of racial injustice and religious intolerance, Christians might take up our faith tradition and tell its stories anew with the hope that it might change the world.

Among the earliest Christians there were storytellers who shared such audacious hope, poets so persuasive that their tales did change the world, orienting not only first-century hearers but somehow shaping worldviews from their day to our own. We might think of these storytellers as the tradition's earliest

theologians, recognizing that "there is no part of the Christian
Scriptures that is not at the same time an expression of a reflec-
tive witness and a believing theology."[1] Telling the story of Jesus,
they wove into their tales answers to life's fundamental questions:
Why are we here? How did we get here? Where are we going?
How will we get there? Their God-talk was determined to per-
suade others to join a movement—a discipleship of equals that
might bring forth a better world.[2]

Among the earliest Christians there were also courageous
activists in this countercultural movement: Phoebe, Prisca, Ju-
nia, and countless other "co-workers, apostles [and] people who
have toiled diligently in the Lord."[3] Shaped by the story of his
life, members of the Jesus movement didn't just read his story,
they did their best to live it: "To learn how to interpret these
scripts well by playing them out in one's life is to learn how to
be a disciple."[4] Living up to the ideals of the movement could
not have been an easy task, so they told and retold the story.
They attempted to be shaped by a life-changing love of God
and neighbor and to embody God's own power in their healing
practices, relational forgiveness, critical judgment, and love of
enemies. In the stories that they told, they imagined that they
had achieved this:

> Awe came upon everyone, because many wonders and signs
> were being done by the apostles. All who believed were

[1] Francis Schüssler Fiorenza, "Systematic Theology: Task and Methods," in *Systematic Theology: Roman Catholic Perspectives*, 2nd ed., ed.
Francis Schüssler Fiorenza and John P. Galvin (Minneapolis: Fortress,
2011), 5.

[2] Elisabeth Schüssler Fiorenza, *In Memory of Her: A Feminist Theological Reconstruction of Early Christian Origins* (New York: Crossroad,
1983).

[3] Elizabeth Castelli, "Romans," in *Searching the Scriptures: A Feminist Commentary*, ed. Elisabeth Schüssler Fiorenza (New York: Crossroad, 1994), 276.

[4] Terrence W. Tilley, *The Disciples' Jesus: Christology as Reconciling
Practice* (Maryknoll, NY: Orbis Books, 2008), 73.

together and had all things in common; they would sell their possessions and goods and distribute the proceeds to all, as any had need. Day by day, as they spent much time together in the temple, they broke bread at home and ate their food with glad and generous hearts, praising God and having the goodwill of all the people. And day by day the Lord added to their number those who were being saved. (Acts 2:43–47)

Resisting affinities with the powers of the world, some found that this countercultural practice and boundary-challenging way of life could speed them to their death. Yet they forged on under the shadow of empire in their refusal to betray the life-giving power of love.

The heart of the Christian story is the person of Jesus, so the Christ-centered focus of Christian theology is not fundamentally the problem. The problem is the use of Jesus Christ as criterion on a sliding scale of humanity and the aligning of Christianity with Whiteness. In order to undo the damage that a White Christian nation has done, we might return to the scriptural sources of our symbolic capital to see if we can mobilize the story of Jesus in a different way.

This mobilization of Christian scripture toward a renewed and antiracist theology rests on the foundational conviction that God is mystery. God is a reality affirmed by the Christian tradition, undeniably, but what God *is* remains beyond human comprehension.[5] Such a Christian orientation affirms that created reality and our creaturely history are both infused with a meaningfulness that finds its source in the creative force that Christians

---

[5] As Thomas Aquinas argues in the *Summa Theologica*, Part I, Q. 2, Art. 1: "We do not know the essence of God." He draws on thinkers from earlier eras, like Pseudo-Dionysius in the sixth century and is taken up by later theologians like Karl Rahner in the twentieth century. For a consideration of this theological theme, see Jeannine Hill Fletcher, *Monopoly on Salvation: A Feminist Approach to Religious Pluralism* (New York: Continuum, 2005), 1–21.

have named God.[6] This is the positive theological affirmation. But the negative limitation on this meaningful source is that, as created human beings, our reach in understanding the creative force (to which we have given the name God) is constrained. This strand of Christian theological affirmation of God's mystery finds precedents in the Jewish tradition and the Hebrew Bible from which Christians draw. God is conceived as the mysterious force of creation that "swept over the face of the water" when the earth was a formless void and darkness covered the face of the deep (Gen 1:2). While we might think of that creative force as a "boundless flowing matter" that exceeds language,[7] humans encountering this creative reality have often expressed the experience in language like "God speaks." In the poetics of human expression humans encounter a creativity beyond themselves and articulate its reality, its presence, and its meaning.

The failures of Christocentrism and the Christian theology that underwrote White supremacy emerge when Christian theology erases the mystery of God through the certainties of a Christ-centered commitment. It is undeniable that Christians have staked the claim that Jesus of Nazareth reveals some reality of the mystery of God, but it is dangerous when this revelation eclipses mystery.[8] In the gospel accounts of Jesus's ministry and teaching, John prefaces the story with the reminder that "no one has ever seen God" (John 1:18) while going on to say that Jesus Christ has made God known. Thus the Christian theological

---

[6] Twentieth-century Christian theologian Gordon Kaufman proposes that the Christian notion of God points to a fundamental creativity in the universe that takes a multiplicity of forms, including human meaning-making (see Gordon Kaufman, *In the Beginning . . . Creativity* [Minneapolis: Augsburg Fortress, 2000]).

[7] Catherine Keller, "Returning God: The Gift of Feminist Theology," in *Feminism, Sexuality, and the Return of Religion*, ed. Linda Martin Alcoff and John Caputo, 55–76 (Bloomington: Indiana University Press, 2011), 62.

[8] For a further discussion of the dual aspects of God's mystery and Jesus as revelation of God, see Roger Haight, *Jesus Symbol of God* (Maryknoll, NY: Orbis Books, 2000).

posture needs to be one of both *mystery* in the ultimate source and power of creation and *meaning* revealed in the person of Jesus. Here is the crucial choice in mobilizing symbolic capital. As we have seen, the meaning of Jesus in the modern era has been to build up White Christians through the denigration and dispossession of non-White, non-Christian others. But surely that is not good news, and we need to mobilize our symbolic capital in other ways.

The symbol set of the New Testament offers a variety of interpretive schemes, and we must choose among them. In mobilizing the witness of Jesus Christ toward undoing White supremacy we might follow the course of Jesus's teaching (as captured in the Gospels) that the central command for a meaningful life, the fullness of life, is love. In what follows I return to the stories of the earliest Christians as resources in the storehouse of symbolic capital to see if there is currency that might be used to construct an antiracist, anti-supremacist understanding of Jesus as the Christ. My proposal is that the persistent claim that *they will know we are Christians by our love* might be a good place to start—reviving ancient wisdoms to critique the epic failure to love that is White supremacy and hoping for patterns for a way forward to love in a weighted world.

In following the life pattern of Jesus, the first storytellers placed love at the heart of their message. Reciting the central teaching of his Jewish faith in God expressed in Torah, Jesus in the Gospels affirms two commandments above all others: love of God and love of neighbor (Matt 22:39; Mark 12:31; Luke 10:27).[9] The earliest Christians recounted this teaching and reminded one another of its centrality, radicalizing the proximal love of neighbor. The apostle Paul wrote to fledgling communities, encouraging them: "The whole law is summed up in a single commandment, 'You shall love your neighbor as yourself'" (Gal 5:14). Paul repeats this in his letters to the ancient Christian

---

[9] Biblical scholarship helps us to see Jesus first as a reformer within the Jewish tradition before he becomes figurehead in the Christian tradition; see Elisabeth Schüssler Fiorenza, *In Memory of Her*, 105–59.

community in Rome: "Owe no one anything, except to love one another; for the one who loves another has fulfilled the law" (Rom 13:8). And in Corinth: "If I have prophetic powers, and understand all mysteries and all knowledge, and if I have all faith, so as to remove mountains, but do not have love, I am nothing" (1 Cor 13:2). Other Christians in antiquity repeat this emphasis: "You do well if you really fulfill the royal law according to the scripture, 'You shall love your neighbor as yourself'" (James 2:8). This proximal love is key to the ultimate meaningfulness of life and creation with its source in the mystery that Christians name God. As one group of early Christians insisted: "Whoever does not love does not know God, for God is love" (1 John 4:8). These two elements of the tradition, the love command of Jesus and the mysteriousness of God, come together in 1 John: "No one has ever seen God; if we love one another, God lives in us and his love is perfected in us" (1 John 4:12). The ultimate meaningfulness of the Christian tradition in drawing out these strands is to affirm the ultimacy of love in and among humanity as participating in the ultimacy of God, that is, the ultimacy of love. In the Christian perspective the mystery of our existence is the mystery of love. The Christian tradition as a love story demonstrates that love is something we work at, something we must craft, and something we desire despite our failings. Is there a possibility of loving after the epic failure to love that is the sin of White Christian supremacy?

Biblical scholar Michael Joseph Brown returns us to one of the most persistent elements of the Christian tradition that reflects the deep desire of love: the Lord's Prayer. These words found in the gospel texts seem to capture the teachings that came from Jesus and express the centrality of love and its continued relevance from the first century to today. In the Lord's Prayer, Christians pray to a God conceived beyond the world ("Our Father in heaven") and who manifests preeminently the sacredness of existence ("hallowed be your name"). Christians orient themselves to the well-being this God designed, not only in a transcendent realm of divine presence, but in everyday existence ("your kingdom come, your will be done, on earth as it is in heaven"). With Jesus, Christians petition that this work of bringing about God's kingdom will encompass human well-being and right relationship ("Give us this day our daily bread, and forgive us our debts, as we also have forgiven our debtors."). Like our forebears who may have heard Jesus recite this prayer, and those who have recited it since, our daily lives are filled with desires that might lead us away from love of God and neighbor, and so our prayer continues, "and do not bring us to the time of trial, but rescue us from evil" (Matt 6:9–13). Brown summarizes the deep logic of love that runs through this prayer:

> Thus, the Christian idea that God is love must move beyond simple agapic language and embrace an erotic understanding as well. The desire to be in relationship—the core of *eros*—is at the core of the Christian message. The petition for the kingdom is more than just a request for a new social ordering. It is an appeal to enact *koinonia*. Yet, it is even more. It is the expression of a desire to be in deep relationship with God. In short, it is erotic.[10]

The Christian call to love, as Brown interprets the Lord's Prayer, includes the selfless love of altruistic behavior toward others but is deeper. The erotic that he draws out illumines a relationship of passionate and intense desire. It is a passionate and intense desire to be in right relationship with others (love of neighbor) and in right relationship with the source of all existence (love of God). The mystery of love that grounds Christian tradition is a mystery of what it means to be human at the deepest level of communion *(koinonia)*, and rests in the simple and yet profound desire to be in relationship, to know, and to experience that we are not alone.

---

[10] Michael Joseph Brown, "The Lure of a Proposition: The Erotic Nature of the Lord's Prayer as Contradiction to Coercive Power," *Interpretation: A Journal of Bible and Theology* 68, no. 1 (2014): 35.

THE GOOD NEWS ACCORDING TO MARK:
LOVE IN THE MODE OF HEALING

While teachings about love have come to be seen as central to Christian tradition, the chronologically first Gospel (Mark) says very little explicitly on the subject.[11] In fact, the topic of love is the articulated center of Jesus's teaching in this story only one time. In chapter 12, in one of many exchanges with religious leaders in this story, "one of the scribes" joined a debate with his own question: "Which commandment is the first of all?" (12:28). Jesus answers with a two-part summary of the heart of the Jewish teaching in Torah, the Shema of Deuteronomy 6:4–5, in which love of God as first commandment cannot be separated from love of neighbor. So, to the scribe's question, Jesus replies: "'Hear, O Israel, the Lord our God, the Lord is one; you shall love the Lord your God with all your heart, and with all your soul, and with all your mind and with all your strength.' And the second is this, 'You shall love your neighbor as yourself.' There is no other commandment greater than these." (12:29–31). In the first and shortest Gospel, in the only instance where Jesus has something to say about love, love of God and neighbor are inseparable.

While only the topic of explicit conversation once, the whole of the Gospel implicitly articulates what this love is about. Loving God and loving neighbor takes on texture when situated in the broader action of the story. We may have come to think of Jesus as the wisdom teacher he becomes in later Gospels, but in this particular Gospel the broader action of the story again and again is healing. As human beings we fail in our capacity to enact

---

[11] While each of the Gospels in the Christian New Testament asserts authorship in the style of "According to Mark" (or Matthew, Luke, or John), many biblical scholars envision these texts emerging from a community process by which the story of Jesus was told over time through a communal narrating process. In that case the story is thought of less as the product of a solitary author and more as a communal story that emerged in response to a group's time, place, questions, and experience.

the well-being for which we were created, and we find ourselves broken. According to Mark, Jesus is one in whom people find the healing that they need. This healing begins with Jesus adopting "a baptism of repentance for the forgiveness of sins" (1:4). And immediately, the one recognized as "beloved" by God experiences a temptation away from God and neighbor. Emergent from this solitary wrestling in the desert and committed in his purpose, Jesus begins a project of calling people to a particular way of being: "repent and believe in the good news" (1:15). A mere twenty-six verses into this story Jesus takes on the characteristic form of love and well-being that will be the hallmark of this Gospel: Jesus drives out an unclean spirit, and his fame as a healer begins to spread. So widespread is his notoriety as a healer that he can no longer move through towns unhindered; people come out to see him in the countryside. He goes through the Gospel healing: a paralytic (2:1–12), a man with a withered hand (3:1–6), the Gerasene demoniac (5:1–20), a woman with a hemorrhage and the daughter of a leader of the synagogue (5:21–43). Jesus travels around the region healing (6:1–13, 30–56) and is challenged by a Syrophonecian woman not to let the boundaries of culture or religion be a barrier to his work (7:24–30). Jesus heals the deaf (7:31–37) and the blind (8:22–26; 10:46–52); he exorcises demons (9:14–29). As a reflection on the world humans actually inhabit, Jesus's world in the Gospel of Mark is full primarily of people who are hurting. They are bleeding, they are withered, they have seizures and spasms, they are estranged, they are dying, they are dead. And the mode through which Jesus loves these neighbors is healing. In addition to the physical acts of healing, Jesus's preaching throughout this Gospel is the healing that comes through the forgiveness of sins. It is forgiveness of sins and healing that are taken up by Jesus's disciples when he sends them on mission, and forgiveness of sins raises suspicion of Jesus on the part of leaders. The love Jesus preaches includes forgiveness, and he encourages those who follow him: "Whenever you stand praying, forgive" (11:25). Healing—of relationships and of persons—is the mode of love most clearly visible in this story.[12] And after all the many healing stories in this Gospel, Jesus is asked by one of the scribes which is the greatest commandment. He answers: "The first is, 'Hear, O Israel: the Lord our God, the Lord is one; you shall love the Lord your God . . . The second is this, 'You shall love your neighbor as yourself.' There is no other commandment greater than these" (12:29–31). When the scribe agrees, Jesus says to him, "You are not far from the kingdom of God" (12:34). The kingdom of heaven looks like the love of God and neighbor that enacts healing in the world. At the closing of the Gospel according to Mark the sign of those who believe and will be saved is that when they lay hands on the sick, those who are hurting recover (16:18).

If the hearer of the story might be tempted to think that love is easy, the story shows that the love that Jesus preaches comes at a cost to those who would follow him. He challenges his listeners to beware of what is offered by those with religious and political power (the yeast of the Pharisees and the yeast of Herod, 8:14–21). To follow Jesus is to relinquish wealth—"Go, sell what you own. . . . Then come, follow me" (10:21). He cautions his listeners to avoid the currency of symbolic capital in glory, honor, credit, praise, and fame when he warns of the model of the scribes being greeted with respect and seeking the best seats in the synagogue and places of honor at banquets. Jesus chastises his disciples when they argue about who among them is the greatest, when they strive to be seated in places of honor. Against the wishes of his companions he chooses the powerless child to be the symbol at the center. To become a disciple of Jesus is to love without regard to the building up of the self and securities: "Whoever wishes to become great among you must be your servant" (10:43); "those who want to save their life will lose it" (8:35).

The chronologically first Gospel in Christian scripture underscores the message that whoever believes in the power of forgiveness and the possibility of healing will be saved (16:16).

---

[12] Elisabeth Schüssler Fiorenza, *In Memory of Her,* 120–21.

Salvation is found in the rejection of status, in the healing of community, and in the forgiveness that comes with the baptism of repentance. The good news in this gospel story is a message of healing, of the power that courses through us in the following of Jesus, who brings with him the rejection of status, the refusal of clinging, the salve that is possible in healing one another, the repentance that is necessary, and the forgiveness that is promised. The sign of those who believe is that they too can perform works of healing in casting out demons, in speaking in new tongues, in facing deadly realities but not being hurt, and in laying hands on the sick for their recovery. Love looks like this.

But love in Mark's Gospel is not a warm, fuzzy feeling. Overall, it is a commitment to a practice even when the way is difficult, even when it is deadly. The dangers of love were written into the story because the earliest Christians had to recount Jesus's life knowing that he had been put to death as an enemy of the state, tortured, and sentenced to crucifixion, an ugly form of slow death not unlike a lynching or execution by a botched injection. As biblical scholar John Meier writes:

> As Jesus the suffering servant descends into the darkness of death without a shred of comfort, we are radically disabused of the modern idea of love as a warm feeling. In the cold darkness of Calvary, covenant love is a matter of doing, not feeling—yes, of doing even when one feels most abandoned and unloved. The commandment of love, as interpreted by Calvary, is a demand for loyalty unto death, joined to a promise of new life beyond and because of one's death to self.[13]

The Gospel according to Mark is a great story of the mystery of love and life. It is a narrative rooted in historical events, telling of a teacher of wisdom and a healer conspired against by

---

[13] John Meier, "Love, in Mark: Christ's Morality of Love" *Mid-Stream* (January 1, 2001), 39.

religious leaders, betrayed by his companions, and put to death by the Roman government. The message of a mystery of love at the depths of injustice is a message that might still have meaning. But as Meier reminds us, the story of Jesus doesn't end with his tragic death. Jesus triumphs over death in the continued presence of his resurrection, which suggests that the love at the center of existence has a vindicating power beyond the evils and tragedies of our world. It's quite remarkable that this story can still function after two thousand years to provide meaning and insight, even in a context very different from the one in which it was written. A broken world needs healing, and the creative power of existence enables that healing to happen through human hands in the world. Could love in the form of healing undo the witchcraft of White supremacy?

THE GOSPEL ACCORDING TO MATTHEW: THE APOCALYPSE OF JUDGMENT

Biblical scholars note that the earliest communities of Christians told the story of Jesus in different ways, tailored to the concerns and experiences of particular audiences. It is not surprising, then, that the portrait of Jesus and the love he proposes might be different when we move to the Gospel according to Matthew. The community from which the Gospel according to Matthew emerged was familiar with the story of Mark and used it as a framework. So, Jesus in the Matthean account is also a healer, but his role as a prophetic teacher is far more pronounced. Expanded in this discussion is the teaching of the kingdom that scholars propose was characteristic of Jesus's message. If the mode of love is healing, then kingdom is the goal. Again and again in this Gospel, Jesus calls his hearers to bring about the kingdom in their lives and in their work.

Like the Gospel according to Mark, very little of Jesus's preaching in Matthew's version expounds explicitly on what love is or does, but a distinctive element in this Gospel indicates to readers something of what love requires. Matthew's Gospel retains a singular focus on Jesus's teaching on the "greatest commandment": love of God and love of neighbor. After Jesus is identified as "the Beloved" at his baptism, Matthew expands on Mark to describe the temptations Jesus faced in the desert (temptations to bread, to safety, and to earthly kingdoms). Then the reader is alerted to a new dimension in Jesus's proclamation to "repent, for the kingdom of heaven has come near" (4:17). The new emphasis that emerges from *repentance* is that it must be followed by *fruits*. Like Mark's Gospel, the baptism Jesus offers entails the confessing of sins, but the focus now is on bearing fruit that is "worthy of repentance" (3:7–8). Repeatedly throughout this Gospel, Jesus announces to his hearers that trees and people will be judged *by their fruits*. Repentance and forgiveness are not relational ideas that manifest in words only; they require new forms of action. Simultaneous to this preaching is the witness to these fruits in the healing of those who are hurting: the leper, the servant, the mother-in-law, the demoniac, the paralytic, the dead daughter, the hemorrhaging woman, the blind, the mute. Jesus "had compassion for them, because they were harassed and helpless" (9:36). It is clear in this Gospel that not everyone is bearing the healing fruit of repentance if some are still harassed and helpless.

Like Mark's account, the Gospel according to Matthew includes Jesus's teaching that the greatest commandment is the dual love of God and neighbor (22:38–40). But almost immediately following this teaching we catch a glimpse of a different portrait of Jesus in relation to this love; that is, Jesus does not just admonish and teach on the commandment to love and enact it in his healing ministry. In the portrait of Jesus in the Gospel of Matthew, Jesus also pronounces judgment on those who fail to enact this love, those who fail to bear the fruits that repentance requires. "Do not do as they do," he warns, "for they do not practice what they teach" (23:3). In expanding upon the failure of prominent members of the religious community, Jesus points to the dangers of a different kind of love. We are to love God and love neighbor, but some "love to have the place of honor at banquet and the best seats in the synagogues and to be greeted with respect in the marketplaces and to have people call them rabbi" (23:6–7). The command is to love God and neighbor, but what many of us love is honor, respect, and recognition, the currency of symbolic capital. This story of Jesus's way of love asks us to ask ourselves, *where is our love directed?* Are we pursuing the self-love of glory, honor, credit, praise, and fame from others? Or is our love directed outward to God and neighbor in relationship? In the antiracist work required of White Christians, will our work be willing to risk the loss of symbolic capital that White supremacy provides?

Matthew's Gospel clearly shows that the possibility for love of God and neighbor when the kingdom draws near is threatened and compromised by different desires in our love. This threat is found in many of the parables this Gospel expands in its building upon Mark: the threat of the weeds that grow up among the wheat (13:24); those who speak good things but are evil (12:34); a whole generation in which "this people's heart has grown dull and their ears are hard of hearing" (13:14). This Gospel presents a much darker portrait of the world, one in which healing is needed because human actions have created evil that structures the world. There are real threats to love's flourishing.

In response to this world of ever-present threat, Jesus's love does not stand idly by. His teaching regularly denounces those whom he sees as masters of evil. "Woe to you, scribes and Pharisees, hypocrites! For you tithe mint, dill, and cummin, and have neglected the weightier matters of the law: justice and mercy and faith. . . . You clean the outside of the cup and of the plate, but inside they are full of greed and self-indulgence" (23:23, 25). The discriminating love of Jesus in this Gospel is rife with judgment: the sheep will be separated from the goats ("you did this to me"), and the goats sent to "eternal punishment" (25:46); the wheat will be removed from the weeds, and the weeds will be burned (13:29). With Jesus's directive to love comes judgment.[14]

---

[14] Ulrich Luz names this "the Matthean theology of judgement" (see Ulrich Luz, "Matthew 21–28: A Commentary," trans. James E. Crouch,

The reality check of Matthew's Gospel is that the right kind of love in biblical perspective is not easy: "The gate is narrow and the road is hard that leads to life" (7:14), *and* there are those who will choose *not* to love in the right way and will be harshly judged. Jesus in this Gospel teaches that wisdom is vindicated by her deeds (11:19) and makes the sharp judgment "whoever is not with me is against me" (12:30). In the parable of the seed sown, we are told that the cares of the world and the lure of wealth choke the word (13:22), and other parables make the point that much must be given up for the kingdom of God (13:44). Once again, witnessing to that love is not easy. Jesus's words in this Gospel state clearly: "If you want to be followers, take up your cross and follow me" (16:24). This Christian message reminds us still, two thousand years later, that love comes at a cost. We may need to give up the places of honor and respect from others; we may need to make difficult decisions that cost us wealth and security. But Jesus in the Gospel according to Matthew asks his followers to love in this way. Might twenty-first-century Christians be willing to pattern their lives in love and to put into practice what Matthew's Jesus teaches?

THE GOSPEL OF LUKE:
THE RADICAL POWER OF LOVE OF ENEMY

When encountering these Gospels one after the other, the reader begins to note places of shared emphasis and places where distinctive ideas are woven into the story by the writer(s) of a given

---

Hermeneia [Minneapolis: Fortress Press, 2005]). See also Andrew Angel, "Inquiring into an *Inclusio*—on Judgement and Love in Matthew," *Journal of Theological Studies* 60, no. 2 (October 2009): 527; John R. Donahue, SJ, "The 'Parable' of the Sheep and the Goats: A Challenge to Christian Ethics," *Theological Studies* 47 (1986): 3–31. Donahue discusses the Christology of Christ as hidden in the suffering other and notes that "apocalyptic is a view of history and human life from God's side" (24).

Gospel. As the early Christian communities made sense of Jesus's story in relation to their lives, they wrote in elements that helped to tell a story that would suit them or challenge their readers. Matthew's Jesus cried woe to the Pharisees; so too does Luke, criticizing the Pharisees as "lovers of money" (16:14) and those who "love to have the seat of honor in the synagogue and to be treated with respect in the marketplaces" (11:43). But there are episodes where Luke's Gospel spreads this woe more generally and insists that not only the Pharisees but *the crowds* must "bear fruit worthy of repentance" (3:7). When John the Baptist warns that Jesus will bring judgment with him, it is notable that he predicts that "every tree, therefore, that does not bear good fruit is cut down and thrown into the fire" (3:9).

Returning to the relationship among healing, loving neighbor, and bearing good fruit, Luke's Jesus is enigmatic and challenging in his refusal to indicate the limits to which one's healing love must extend. Throughout the Gospels, Jesus is challenged in his teaching and returns regularly to the central teaching of the Shema: love God and love neighbor. Yet, in one particular exchange the challenge extends further as Jesus's questioner asks, "Who is my neighbor?" (Luke 10:29). Jesus refuses to give a direct answer and instead tells the story of a Samaritan who finds a man beaten and robbed by the side of the road, his pious countrymen having refused to help him. The expansive scope of the love of neighbor expands in both Matthew's and Luke's Gospels to a countercultural, radical love that extends beyond natural ties of kinship and tribe. In Matthew's Gospel Jesus taught, "Love your enemies. . . . For if you love those who love you, what reward do you have?" (5:44, 46). Luke's Gospel repeats this teaching with an extended meditation: "Love your enemies, do good to those who hate you, bless those who curse you, pray for those who abuse you. . . . If you love those who love you, what credit is that to you? For even sinners love those who love them. . . . But love your enemies, do good, and lend, expecting nothing in return" (6:27, 32, 35). It is as if placing love in the place least expected brings the greater reward, just as forgiveness to the one with many sins has an exponential effect. In one episode of Jesus's healing through forgiveness, the storytellers have him say: "Therefore, I tell you, her sins, which were many, have been forgiven; hence she has shown great love. But the one to whom little is forgiven, loves little" (Luke 7:47). There is a reciprocal effect here of love of enemy and forgiveness, where the one who receives these gifts/graces—who receives them even when disproportionately undeserving—is able to give them in return.

The seemingly mysterious project of love of enemy invites us to consider once again the relationship between love of God and love of neighbor, precisely in the possibility that a love that extends to even the despised neighbor is a powerful tool for the healing of the world. As Aaron Kuecker interprets the gospel message, "Jesus's defeat of his enemies comes not through death-dealing violence but through enemy love and radical generosity."[15] Luke's treatment of enemy love proposes that the power to defeat through love is a human reality that brings us close to the divine: "But love your enemies, do good, and lend, expecting nothing in return. Your reward will be great, and you will be sons of the Most High; for he is kind to the ungrateful and the wicked. Be merciful just as your Father is merciful" (Luke 6:35–36). If God is love, and Jesus manifests the mystery of God, then Jesus's characteristics of love demonstrate his likeness to God through enemy love and radical generosity. And in this passage from Luke, these are the characteristics Jesus calls his followers to so that they also might become "sons of the Most High." Kuecker writes, "Followers of Jesus can share Jesus' identity as son of the Most High as they follow Jesus into enemy love and radical generosity, for to adopt that pattern of life is to be conformed to the life of the Most High."[16]

---

[15] Aaron Kuecker, "'You Will Be Children of the Most High': An Inquiry into Luke's Narrative Account of Theosis," *Journal of Theological Interpretation* 8, no. 2 (2014): 215.

[16] Ibid., 219.

The proximal love of neighbor and enemy brings us as close as possible to the ultimate mystery of existence as the mystery of love. These forms of love are a mystery and a challenge, but one can see the possibilities of this wisdom in transforming a world broken by division. The remarkable relevance of an ancient wisdom is once again an invitation to twenty-first-century seekers after a meaningful life and those compelled toward a world of racial justice and religious diversity. What would it look like if Christian congregations mobilized the radical power of love of enemy for the healing of our world?

THE GOSPEL OF JOHN:
THE FOUNDATIONS OF LOVE IN INTIMACY

Among all four Gospels, the most extensive and repeated discussion of love is in the Gospel according to John. But given what we have seen with the radical outlook of love of enemy, love manifest in this Gospel might feel quite narrowly construed. In the Gospel according to John the topic of love is returned to regularly, but its most visible manifestation is as a relationship that is cultivated between individuals. For example, the way Jesus loves particular people in the stories of Mary, Martha, and their brother, Lazarus (12—13), or in the way one among the disciples is described as the disciple whom Jesus loved (21), suggests love with a somewhat narrow scope. The love that John's Jesus communicates in this Gospel seems to be an intense and sustained love, but it might also be a love within limits. The nature of this love as intimate, as sustained by relationship, and as developed over time does seem to be a mode of being in the world that makes distinctions among its objects. That Jesus loved Lazarus in a particular way underscores a differentiated relationship, different from what Jesus had with others; similarly, the point of identifying the disciple whom Jesus loved is to set that disciple rhetorically apart from the others. When Jesus expands the relationship of love that flows between himself and God, it flows in and among his disciples, but not necessarily (yet) flowing out indiscriminately into the world. The primary characteristic of love in John's rendering is *intimacy in relationship.*

It is this intimate love that Jesus bestows as a command on his disciples in his farewell discourses at the end of John's Gospel. In the evening of the last supper, before he is to be betrayed, tortured, and crucified, he tells his most intimate group of companions: "Love one another as I have loved you" (15:12). The nature of love as intimacy is important to grasp here, so I quote this gospel farewell at length. Jesus says to his companions:

> "As the Father has loved me, so I have loved you; abide in my love. If you keep my commandments, you will abide in my love, just as I have kept my Father's commandments and abide in his love. I have said these things to you so that my joy may be in you, and that your joy may be complete.
>
> "This is my commandment, that you love one another as I have loved you. No one has greater love than this, to lay down one's life for one's friends. You are my friends if you do what I command you. I do not call you servants any longer, because the servant does not know what the master is doing; but I have called you friends, because I have made known to you everything that I have heard from my Father. You did not choose me but I chose you. And I appointed you to go and bear fruit, fruit that will last, so that the Father will give you whatever you ask him in my name. I am giving you these commands so that you may love one another." (John 15:9–17)

A deep and abiding intimacy is what Jesus bequeaths to those who have followed him. Jesus prays these words, desiring that the intimate love for God might envelop also his closest companions:

> As you, Father, are in me and I am in you, may they also be in us, so that the world may believe that you have sent me. The glory that you have given me I have given them, so that they may be one, as we are one, I in them and you

in me, that they may become completely one, so that the world may know that you have sent me and have loved them even as you have loved me. (17:21–23)

In returning to this Gospel and noticing the limits of this love in its discriminating function, a reader might find this narrow or constricted, given what we have seen of a love that flows out into the world for radical and unexpected healing. But John's rendition of Jesus's love and his exhortation to love intimately is a reminder that even our closest relationships are ones that are tested by the challenges to love, the challenges of intimacy. Love, then, is a relational reality that needs feeding in both intimate and public ways. As we activate Christian love in the world to neighbor and enemy, we are reminded to foster the mysterious bonds of intimacy that might sustain our work.

DIVERSITY IN THE FORMS OF LOVE

In contemplating a pattern of Christian love from the New Testament that we can follow, I propose that we read the Gospels in a chronologically reverse order to build a notion of love from intimacy in concentric circles into the world. As we have seen, John's Gospel (the last one written) has a rich and extensive vision of intimate love among the followers of Jesus. We might rest with this conception of love to recognize that indeed love is cultivated in intimate relationships—with those whom we share our everyday lives, who stay with us over the passage of time, who become woven into our very being. A Christian conception of love includes this radical intimacy, and with the help of the social sciences, psychology, and practical experience, we can explore the depths of how difficult this intimate love really is. With the invitation to begin in commitments of love in close proximity, the Christian call seeks relational well-being on many levels.

But love cannot be limited to this radical intimacy. The networks of intimate love relationships ought to follow the pattern of Jesus's farewell discourses so that the love that flows between two might flow out to enliven others. Here we need to expand from John's rendering to incorporate also the gospel accounts of its historical predecessors. From intimate love we might extend to the love of neighbor that runs through the Gospels. Love of God and neighbor is not simply intimate love, but a love that turns outward to the world. Here the judgment of Matthew's Gospel might be a helpful reminder that love turned outward can find expression in ways that are not useful: in love of power, prestige, money. But, following the trajectory, the flow of love through the Gospels includes Mark's healing love, a love that sustains the rebuilding of persons and the world by its presence. Mark's healing accounts of love are not intimate—they are expressions of love even among strangers—but they are expressions of love in the form of healing. To these expanding venues of love from intimacy out into the world, we need to include Luke's love of enemy. That is, the Christian might be formed in close ties of intimacy, where this love expands out into the world for healing, but Christian love is incomplete without the countercultural love of enemy that Luke's Gospel announces.

Love in the gospel accounts takes these many forms, and a Christian witness to love cannot be reduced to any one. As a story with remarkable challenges twenty centuries later, we might ask: How do we cultivate relationships of intimacy where love binds us particularly to some over others, and at the same time expand that love out into the world in a healing presence, expanding that love even to our "enemy"? Are there limits to our love? Here, returning to the bond of human and divine love is essential to the Christian perspective. If God is love, and ultimate Source of all that is, and humans participate in that boundless creativity of love, then we might be invited to consider our capacity for love as boundless. No matter the failures of our intimacy, the shortcomings of our healing, the refusals of our love of enemy, the boundless Source calls us to ever greater realization that love remains available.

Guided by the concentric circles of love presented in the Gospels, twenty-first-century Christians might still ask how they are to express Christian love in the world: How do I foster bonds of intimacy and allow that intimate love to flow out into my encounters with others in the world? How am I a healer? How do I bear fruit worthy of repentance? How do I show compassion to the harassed and helpless? How do I forego the love of money, fame, honor, and titles? How do I forgive and enact even love of my enemy? The call of the Gospel and Christian love in the world are incomplete without these various forms enacted.

THE EPIC FAILURE OF CHRISTIANS TO LOVE

A return to New Testament stories and the centrality of love in Christian tradition stands in stark contrast to the epic failure of love that is White Christian supremacy. Instead of a love of other that extended across boundaries and borders, Christian theo-logic in America cultivated the self-love of White supremacy. For those Christians compelled by the injustice of structural White supremacy and seeking a way forward, the gospel witness to love might still be compelling. The question, however, is not only how do we love, but how do we love after the witchcraft of White supremacy? How do we love in a world weighted with disparity when White Americans enjoy the benefits of exploitation and people of color continue to bear its weight?

The Christian witness to love embedded in the symbolic capital of New Testament stories can be written forward with the help of the longer tradition of Christian reflection. Continuing to tell the story of Jesus in new times and places, Christians throughout the centuries have bequeathed to us additional resource in the storehouse of symbolic capital. Looking for a witness to love that might orient us away from Christian supremacy, we look to Christology again for alternative meanings.

5

CHRIST CRUCIFIED

CLAIMS OF CHRIST'S SUPREMACY HAVE underwritten ideologies of White supremacy. But given the centrality of Jesus, Christians cannot simply relinquish Christ in their quest for a non-supremacist theology. At the same time, Christ must function in a new way, not as root criterion for the sliding scale of humanity but as mirror and model for a Christian way of being human in light of the mystery that is love. Jesus Christ is my way of being human—he transforms those who follow him from self-centeredness toward the possibilities of love—but there are other ways of being human, other mirrors and models of loving. Humanity, in all its diversity, is not enacting a sliding scale of sufficiency and deficiency along God's singular continuum. Humanity, in all its diversity, reflects back to us the mystery that we remain to ourselves and the endless possibilities that reside within the creative force at the heart of reality. This creative force Christians have called God and have named love. Holding my claims to truth lightly, recognizing the way Christ and Christian claims have functioned in the past toward discrimination and dehumanization, Christ is the answer for me, but in a particular way. Christ is the Crucified One who radiates love against the backdrop of mystery.

This Christ is intimately revealed in the historical person of Jesus of Nazareth, in the flesh-and-blood life, ministry, and death of a first-century Jew. Even two thousands years later it seems relevant that this man thought that we human beings have the potential for love. In the stories of the New Testament, Jesus sees that things could be different if people would return to the deep wisdom of Jewish teaching in Torah and abide by the dual promise of life in love of God and love of neighbor. As remembered in Luke's Gospel, Jesus was someone who visioned what it was to turn from self-centeredness and encourage greater kindness and flexibility. In one particular episode the most skillful of reasoners (a lawyer) asked the fundamental question about the ultimate goal of human existence: "Teacher, what must I do to inherit eternal life?" With patience (or perhaps losing patience) Jesus reflects the question back to his questioner: "What is written in the law?" Of course, they both knew this deep wisdom. The lawyer answered without missing a beat, "You shall love the Lord your God with all your heart, and with all your soul, and with all your strength, and with all your mind; and your neighbor as yourself" (Luke 10:25–27). *Good*, we can almost hear Jesus say, *now let's go and do that*. The abiding principle Jesus drew from his Jewish tradition and passed on is love; these guidelines will lead us from out of our self-centeredness into greater circles of kindness. Amazingly, the ancient wisdom continues to be relevant for us today. Love of the Source at the center of the universe and love of others might lead us out from our self-centeredness and into loving-kindness, community, and the experience of not being alone.

But the stories that are told about Jesus as they come to us in the Gospels remind us of our human desire to set limits to our love. Like us, the lawyer presses the issue, intellectualizing the directive with further argumentation to try to pin down the truth of love. "And who is my neighbor?" he asks. As evidenced in the lawyer's response and the history of Christianity's epic failures to love, even the capacious direction to loving-kindness that turns us out from ourselves to God and others can be inflexible in its legalized application. Like the mystery of love itself, Jesus responds with a story that is confounding and confusing but might render love more flexible. He tells the parable of the good

Samaritan. In this story we see a love that loves across boundaries of difference and cares intimately for the religious and racial other. To the Samaritan, the stranger whom he saw bloodied at the side of the road and whom he bandaged to begin his healing was religiously and culturally outside the boundaries of his community.[1] The example Jesus gives of the kind of life that is salvific is one that loves and cares across lines of difference.

We might need to pause at this point to consider how a healing presence across lines of difference might be a transgressive reality. The constructions of difference often serve materially to shore up and secure capital that is both symbolic and economic. Through the logic of identity "we" create a world with "us" in it, and name through symbolic capital those within the scope of our concern. With the value-laden opposition of "us" and "other," affirmation is established insofar as we/us constitute the horizon of our concern. We need to ensure that *we* are cared for, afforded the necessities of well-being, and a life truly human. That the other is other is precisely why they are not our principal concern. "They," the other, need to secure well-being for themselves. But the story of the good Samaritan captures Jesus's transgressive behavior. Just as the despised Samaritan brought the Jewish Other into the horizon of his healing, Jesus repeatedly throughout the Gospels brings his healing across boundaries, even boundaries of "enemy" others. Even as he challenges imperial power, he heals the beloved of the centurion. Even as he challenges religious power, he heals the daughter of the synagogue's leader. He heals across boundaries of nation in encountering the Syrophonecian woman; he heals the diseased and despised. Challenging the status quo of symbolic capital assigned to places of honor, he shared meals with those who had dishonor heaped upon them: tax collectors and sinners. It was from this sort of transgressive action

---

[1] Historical perspective indicates that Samaritans were distinct from Jews both religiously and ethnically. This lends itself to thinking parallel to our discussion of a religio-racial project. On this, see R. J. Coggins, *Samaritans and Jews: The Origins of Samaritanism Reconsidered* (Oxford: Basil Blackwell, 1975).

that the earliest Christians affirmed: "There is no longer Jew or Greek, there is no longer slave or free, there is no longer male and female; for all of you are one in Christ Jesus" (Gal 3:28).

While the Christian call across boundaries is clear, structures and systems also rely on the creation of the other for maintaining the limits of concern, the reach of responsibility for recognition, rights, and well-being in the imagined space of scarce resources. The transgressive healings recounted in the New Testament reflect the kinds of teachings and activities that might be challenging to the guardians of symbolic capital. Their message pushes against the boundaries of established norms and laws, since boundaries—both political and religious—set the parameters for order. As New Testament scholar Warren Carter articulates, in conspiring to bring Jesus to his death, "the [local religio-political] Jerusalem rulers and the [imperial] Roman governor work together to remove a provincial who is challenging the imperial order."[2] Loving God and neighbor in ways that dismantled the boundaries that maintained power and privilege brought many among the powerful and privileged to desire Jesus's disposal. The gospel accounts indicate how difficult it is to love in a weighted world, because the story of Jesus as lover of humanity across lines of difference is simultaneously the story of Jesus as threat to the established order of religious authoritarianism and political dominations. It's not that the story of the good Samaritan was blasphemous and led directly to Jesus's murder, but it reflects ideas and practices that did.

The Christ who is my way, truth, and life, is the one who comes to us as the tortured teacher of an authentic way of being human that challenges privilege in the past and remains challenging today. Christ comes to us not only as teacher of a boundless love that loves across borders, but he comes to us also as the Crucified One. The teacher of Christian ways rooted in Jewish

---

[2] Warren Carter, "Matthew Negotiates the Roman Empire," in *In the Shadow of Empire: Reclaiming the Bible as a History of Faithful Resistance*, ed. Richard Horsley (Louisville, KY: Westminster John Knox Press, 2008), 123.

wisdom comes to us simultaneously as the one who gives life with his healing presence and the one who takes on the death dealt through the refusal to love. As liberation theologian Ignacio Ellacuría writes:

> Jesus dies—is killed as the four gospels and Acts so insist—because of the historical life he led, a life of deeds and words that those who represented and held the reins of the religious, socioeconomic, and political situation could not tolerate. . . . The activity, word, and very person of Jesus in the proclamation of the Reign [of God] were so assertive and so against the established order and basic institutions that they had to be punished by death.[3]

When agents of the Roman Empire put to death an activist Jew, the cross on Calvary served the purposes of torture and terror: torture for the one accused of treason to the established order, and terror for those who witnessed it. For those who would challenge the unjust status quo and the many political, economic, and religious institutions that sustained it, the message was sent that to disrupt the balance of power in a weighted world could be deadly. In the claim that God resides in Jesus Christ, Christians have said that love looks like this. There is no greater love than to lay down one's life for one's friends by challenging unjust systems, since the boundaries of who is a friend is an ever-receding horizon that encompasses the totality of bodies in our weighted world. This is love in a weighted world.

Historical methods point to the power structures of empire and its tools as ultimately responsible for death by crucifixion. But the gospel writers spread more widely the responsibility for Jesus's death. In the Gospel according to Luke, both Pilate and Herod (the agents of empire) exonerate Jesus and seek his release.

---

[3] Ignacio Ellacuría, "The Crucified People: An Essay in Historical Soteriology," in *Ignacio Ellacuría: Essays on History, Liberation, and Salvation*, ed. Michael E. Lee (Maryknoll, NY: Orbis Books, 2013), 206–7.

It is the crowds of people who insist on his death. Luke seems to be saying that responsibility for crucifixion must be shared among the many parties who benefit from the systems of power that keep boundaries of well-being firmly in place. In this version of the story, while key individuals were willing to allow Jesus's message of boundary-crossing love to live, the majority of those invested in the status quo of a weighted world refused.

Thus the cross of Christ does not point only to powerful empires as death-dealing; the Crucified One indicts a much wider range of human participation in systems and structures that kill. Luke's crowds shouting, "Crucify, crucify him!" (23:21) place *us* at the foot of the cross, indicted for the many ways we have been the crucifiers. In the words of Swiss Reformed theologian Karl Barth, Jesus Christ is "the point at which is perceived the crimson thread which runs through all history" reflecting back to us from the cross the depths of our sinful condition and saving us from our violent mistreatment of our others.[4] That crimson thread includes those places where Christians have taken the cross as the instrument by which to torture and put to death those they viewed as others. The crimson thread is seen whenever the limits of our love are death-dealing.

The affirmation that God becomes human in the crucified Jesus is a theological assertion that God does not reside in some disaffected realm away from the world, but that God cares for creation in an intimate way. In the creative action that brought forth the world that is good, God is the mystery that sustains the earth and what is in it. Further, the affirmation that God resides within the torture victim places God on the side of the dispossessed rather than the powerful. In taking up residence in the body of the victim of state-sanctioned torture, supported by the power that circulates through widespread human participation in systems that kill, Christian faith asserts that the creative force of God seeks the goodness of *all* and not just the well-being of

---

[4]Karl Barth, *The Epistle to the Romans*, translated from the sixth edition by Edwyn C. Hoskyns (London: Oxford University Press, [1933] 1968), 96.

some. The message of Christ crucified has multiple meanings in Christian tradition, but among them is that the creative power of well-being drives across humanly constructed boundaries even when those invested in those boundaries mount the power to crush God's life-infusing presence. Jesus enacts God's well-being in his life and through his death, as the moment through which we see the arc of the universe bending toward justice. Even as his body is lifted in torture, pierced by the soldier's sword, bleeding from his thorn-torn brow and nail-punctured hands and feet, Christian faith is placed in the triumph over destruction that resurrection promises. The affirmation that God resides in Jesus is the affirmation that resident within the body broken and bloodied by the weight of the world, God abides with the tortured and transforms death to new life.

God lives within the body of the tortured and through the Crucified One. Christians are called back to the pattern of love that fundamentally challenges any limits to universal human well-being, any limits to Christian love. Abiding with those crushed by the weight of the world, God resides in Baltimore, and in Ferguson, and on the South Side of Chicago, where generations of White supremacy and White Christian ideologies have shifted the weight of the world. Abiding with those crushed by the weight of the world, God resides on the US-Mexico border, where God's creative life blood sends people across the desert in their struggle for well-being. Abiding with those crushed by the weight of the world, God resides with the family of Deah Shaddy Barakat, Yusor Mohammad, and Razan Mohammad Abu-Salha. God resides in the cells of prisoners at Guantanamo, today's victims of state-sanctioned torture who cry out:

> They leave us in prison for years, uncharged
> Because we are Muslims.
> Where is the world to save us from torture?[5]

---

[5] Adnan Farhan Abdul Latif, "Hunger Strike Poem," *Poems from Guantánamo,* ed. Marc Falkoff (Iowa City: University of Iowa, 2007), 52.

God resides on the reservation in the despairing teen and the advocate who fights for her. How long the list goes on, the places where God resides, among the dispossessed denounced by a White Christian nation. In gazing upon the Crucified One, Christians should ask themselves, *In what ways have I contributed to the weight of the world and in what ways have I tortured others?* In what ways have I contributed to the crimson thread that runs through history, compromising God's creative life presence and putting to death the God resident among us? How haunting the reminder of the sins of White supremacy is the image of Christ crucified.

A GHOSTLY GRACE

In Christian tradition the symbol of Christ crucified—the sign of the cross—is a witness to the ways that humanity is responsible for the death-dealing weight of the world that puts love to death. Christians willing to take responsibility for our participation in the death-dealing currents of power and sinful action might be called to self-awareness repeatedly in gazing upon the cross. Standing at the foot of the cross, Christians are indicted for their death-dealing in the name of Christ.

But in the stories of Christian tradition Jesus Christ does not remain a passive object of contemplation resident on the instrument of state-sanctioned torture. Christ lives! The story of the Christian tradition continues in the New Testament accounts when those who followed him in his life continue to experience him among them after his death. This is the story of resurrection, when the healing power that courses through creation and enlivened Jesus of Nazareth could not be contained in the body of his earthly, historical life. His earthly existence was transformed as it was taken up into the creative power of God. Jesus is not a past reality in Christian thought and practice but a continuing reality in and through the life of the believer. In the stories of the Gospels, Jesus visits his followers after his death, surprising and confusing them, but ultimately empowering them to continue his life-giving work.

Christian tradition articulates this continued presence as life in the resurrection—as Jesus Christ conquers death. In the words of the Apostles' Creed ancient Christians expressed a belief that the one who died under state-sanctioned torture was not diminished by the power of death:

> He suffered under Pontius Pilate,
>   was crucified, died, and was buried.
> He descended to the dead.
> On the third day he rose again.
> He ascended into heaven,
>   and is seated at the right hand of the Father.
> He will come again to judge the living and the
>   dead.

While Christian empire has extoled the virtues of Christ-victor "seated at the right hand of the Father" and mobilized this symbolic capital for death-dealing ends, another thread of the tradition might be teased out with the idea that Jesus "comes again" as judge. The love Jesus extolled in the New Testament—healing, loving even enemies, and intimacy—came with love as judgment as well, and this, too, cannot be conquered by death.

The thread of Christ as judge coming again (and again) to haunt the living can be seen in the visits of Christ upon the mystics of the Middle Ages. For these Christians, Jesus was not only a first-century Jew but a presence among them, visiting them in their deepest contemplation to witness the power of God coursing through creation, but also bringing the judgment of God on human failings. In the presence of Jesus visited upon the mystics, God's love and judgment, justice, and mercy are held together in symbolisms that flourished in the seventeenth-century devotion to the sacred heart. This strand of symbolism, which draws the believer into the broken heart of Jesus, has earlier precedents in the mystical visions of Mechtild of Hackeborn in the thirteenth century. Her collected works provide us with the lens through which to view her encountering the "ghostly grace" of Christ's haunting presence.[6] When Mechtild shares the haunting visited upon her, she hones in on the cross as true salvation.[7] In the cross of Christ, she saw the "wound of love"—the ultimate expression of pouring oneself out in love for the world.[8] The heart broken by the cross remains a source of the grace of love. His heart is like an ever-flowing oil lamp by which others are enlivened; his heart is as a cup to be shared and to drink from.[9] What flows from the "spice-chest" of the divine heart is the salve that heals the wounds of humanity. Mechtild expressed the desire that

> He Who said, "If I shall be lifted up from earth, I will draw all things unto Me," may draw thy heart, with all the powers of thy soul, to Himself, and make thee to run with love and desire to the odour of those ointments which have flowed in such abundance from the noble spice-chest of His Heart, that they have filled heaven and earth.[10]

Deep contemplation of Jesus draws us into his heart as source of love from which Christians draw. Attention to the heart as an embodied reality communicates the presence of God in the created world (the sacramental) as it draws us into the material heart, the vital organ that beats in real bodies and in Jesus's real body. Sacramentality and incarnation draw together the human

---

[6] A translation error from the original German writing of her *Book of Special Graces* was rendered in Middle English as *The Booke of Gostlye Grace* (see *The Booke of Gostlye Grace of Mechtild of Hakeborn*, ed. Theresa A. Halligan [Toronto: Pontifical Institute of Medieval Studies, 1979]).

[7] Medieval Library of Mystical and Ascetical Works, *Select Revelations of S. Mechtild, Virgin, Taken from the Five Books of Her Spiritual Grace and Translated from the Latin by a Secular Priest* (London: Thomas Richardson and Sons, 1875), 33.

[8] Ibid., 40.

[9] Ibid., 137.

[10] Ibid., 177–78.

Christ and ourselves as human beings, so that the deepest truths we witness in the person of Jesus are truths that reflect back to us who *we* are to be. Doctor of the church Bernard of Clairvaux (1090–1153) connected the humanity of Christ with our humanity through the heart, seeing "the heart as the place within the person where God is to be found."[11] As Jesus visits upon Christians his "ghostly grace," they experience themselves connected through hearts that beat by the grace of God.

The heart, in the Gospel of John and the letters of Paul in the New Testament, stands in for and reflects back to us a sign of Jesus's love. But the specific, embodied kind of love that Jesus's heart witnesses is important. Linked with the pierced side at the crucifixion (John 19:34) this heart is one that was wounded and broken. Bonaventure in the thirteenth century says it this way: "The Heart of our Lord was pierced with a lance, that by the visible wound we might recognize the invisible love."[12] When the sacred heart appears in Catholic symbolism, it is the image of a heart that is pierced and bleeding. It is a heart bound by the torturer's thorns, like barbed wire, and bleeding from the torturer's sword. This sacred heart is a heart broken by love—by the rejection of love, by the refusal of love—on the part of those who refuse to carry on love in the world as much as on the part of those who killed Jesus.

The sacred heart image shows Jesus pointing to his heart or the heart encircled by thorns standing alone. The heart is sometimes rendered anatomically with veins encircling it; sometimes it is pierced; sometimes it bleeds. It is accompanied by a great flame and the cross itself, instrument of torture, emerging from it. The sacred heart imagery is of love and torture; it brings us in

---

[11] Jeanne Weber, "Devotion to the Sacred Heart: History, Theology, and Liturgical Celebration," *Worship* 72, no. 3 (May 1, 1998): 239. Note the paradox that Bernard was both drawn to the deep humanity of Jesus through the sacred heart *and* did not see the humanity of others as he preached the Second Crusade in 1145.

[12] Bonaventure, *Vitis Mystica*, cited in Weber, "Devotion to the Sacred Heart," 242.

to the real life blood and bodies that break from torture. It harkens back to the heart that haunted the mystic Mechtild. As her biographer reports: "One day our Lord appeared to Mechtilde as though suspended, with hands and feet tied, and said to her: 'Every time a man sins mortally he ties Me thus, and as long as he perseveres in his sin he keeps Me in this torture.'"[13] If we were to allow the sacred heart of Jesus to continue to haunt Christians today, we might be pressed to ask again and again, where is the Crucified One now kept in a state of torture? Where does the pierced heart of Jesus break for the brokenness of our world?

In answering, we return again to wholeness in order to know where brokenness reigns. In the words of *Gaudium et Spes:*

> There must be made available to all men everything necessary for leading a life truly human, such as food, clothing, and shelter; the right to choose a state of life freely and to found a family; the right to education, to employment, to a good reputation, to respect, to appropriate information, to activity in accord with the upright norm of one's conscience, to protection of privacy, and to rightful freedom in matters religious too. (no. 26)

If this is the vision the tradition holds forth as the narrative of the fullness of humanity, how does the sacred heart of Jesus break when these are not made available? Who is it that struggles for food, clothing, shelter? Where does the sacred heart of Jesus break at the refusal of education, employment, a good reputation, privacy, respect? How does it break for those denied their rightful freedom of religion? On nearly every measure of our American landscape, the vision put forth by *Gaudium et Spes* disproportionately is refused to men, women, and children of color; it is regularly refused to men, women, and children who are guided by the wisdom traditions and religious practices of

---

[13] *The Love of the Sacred Heart, Illustrated by St. Mechtilde, with a Foreword by the Lord Bishop of Salford* (London: Burns, Oates and Washbourne, 1922), 125.

non-Christian faiths. The broken heart of Jesus breaks for *this* world, where the ideology of White supremacy has created historical institutions from which White Americans continue to benefit at the expense of people of color and the exclusion of our neighbors of other faiths. As we have seen, these disparities were not accidental. They were carefully crafted by a nation's history of dispossession, where the interests of White Christians prevailed in death-dealing programs for others. From the revolution to the Civil War, American institutions were forged with the interests of White Christians at the fore, and the formation of America as a White Christian nation came by way of genocide, conversion away from indigenous religions, and the suppression of native African practices among those enslaved to build the country.[14] The continued dispossession of the natives of this land and exploitation of the enslaved were political projects designed to build up a White Christian nation as a beacon of God's favor. In the reconstruction of the United States after the Civil War, systems of White supremacy in Jim Crow laws and the lynching era continued to control Black and Brown bodies in the name of White morality and social order. Asian Americans were excluded from citizenship in the name of the Christian God.[15] Economic dispossessions were planned actions in the restrictions of social security, racist lending, and mortgage practices, while infusing government resources into White suburbs; all of this bears a historical weight on our present conditions. The courage of Native American activists and so many in the civil rights movements to break these systems of oppression stands alongside the reality of White oppressors refusing to give up their privileges (and often

---

[14] For a concise overview of this history, see Joseph Barndt, *Becoming an Anti-Racist Church: Journeying toward Wholeness* (Minneapolis: Augsburg Fortress, 2011), 23–67.

[15] Daniel B. Lee, "A Great Racial Commission: Religion and the Construction of White America," in *Race, Nation, and Religion in the Americas*, ed. Henry Goldschmidt and Elizabeth McAlister, 85–110 (New York: Oxford University Press, 2004), 87. See also James Cone, *The Cross and the Lynching Tree* (Maryknoll, NY: Orbis Books, 2011).

using religious symbolisms to do so). These are the historical oppressions that have given way to structural inequalities along race lines. The broken heart of Jesus breaks for *this* world, for *our* world, where Black and Brown Christians and others are humiliated, incarcerated, dehumanized, and rejected at our borders and within our borders.

In revisiting the tradition of Christ's haunting visions in the visitation to the mystics, we might envision the function of Christ as savior haunting Christians to enact Christian love. Devotion to the sacred heart rests with the crown of thorns as an instrument of torture and requires that we interrogate our own complicity in the sins of White supremacy—in what we have done and in what we have failed to do. The haunting of St. Lutgarde (b. 1182) saw the Virgin Mary in sorrow for the ways Christians were once again crucifying Jesus.[16]

In contemplating the Crucified One the torture victim resident in our holy spaces, and the continuing torture of the sacred heart of Jesus, we return to the story of resurrection. The Christian story doesn't end with the death of Jesus but narrates the next chapter as one in which Jesus is encountered by those who followed him as a presence among them after his death. It is the ghosts of the crucified people that haunt us as Christ's presence among us. In the words of Ignacio Ellacuría,

> What is meant by the crucified people here is that collective body, which as the majority of humankind owes its situation of crucifixion to the way society is organized and maintained by a majority that exercises its dominion through a series of factors, which taken together and given their concrete impact within history, must be regarded as sin.[17]

---

[16] Thomas Merton, *What Are These Wounds: The Life of a Cistercian Mystic, Saint Lutgarde of Aywières*, reprint ed. (Mahwah, NJ: Paulist Press, 2015).

[17] Ignacio Ellacuría, "The Crucified People," in *Systematic Theology: Perspectives from Liberation Theology*, ed. Jon Sobrino and Ignacio Ellacuría (Maryknoll, NY: Orbis Books, 1996), 266.

In the enslaved mothers who saw their babies sold, Christ haunts as the Crucified One who stands in judgment over White Christians. In the others whose lives are disrupted and denied by White Christian supremacies, the crucified people once again witness the persistent presence of Christ: Native Americans and other indigenous peoples, victims of the lynching tree and systemic police violence, prisoners at Guantánamo, the Chinese unworthy of becoming citizens. The cross of Christ and the crucified people function to reveal how the sin of White Christian supremacy has inflicted death in the name of Christ's eternal life.

It is not only Christ's sacred heart that breaks for those who are broken and tortured; our hearts must break as well. They must be wounded with love. Bernard of Clairvaux's *Sermon on the Song of Songs* asks us to be pierced by the piercing love of Jesus.[18] "'A polished arrow' too is that special love of Christ. . . . I would reckon myself happy if at rare moments I felt at least the prick of the point of that sword. Even if only bearing love's slightest wound, I could say, 'I am wounded with love.'"[19] Our hearts must break for our neighbors of other faiths, denied their rights and their freedom of expression. The sacred heart of Jesus breaks and ours must also for the Christian politicians who name Muslims "enemy" and work to restrict their access to and freedom within this country.[20] We need not look far to see the practices in our world that refuse human well-being. With Bernard, our hearts should feel some prick of the excruciating pain as the sword buried into Christ's flesh as crucifixion continues today. Through a common piercing of the sacred heart of Jesus, twenty-first-century Christians might experience what twelfth-century

---

[18] Franz Posset, "Saint Bernard of Clairvaux in the Devotion, Theology, and Art of the Sixteenth Century," *Lutheran Quarterly* 11 (September 1997): 316.

[19] Bernard of Clairvaux, *Sermons on the Song of Songs,* Sermon 29, IV.8.

[20] Matt Katz, "What South Carolina Republicans Want to Hear from Christie (Should He Run)," *New Jersey Public Radio,* September 17, 2014, http://www.wnyc.org. This rhetoric escalated in the 2016 presidential election campaigns.

mystics described as an "infused love" made visible. Modern-day mystic Thomas Merton explains: "Stigmata, for St. John of the cross, are simply external wounds which sometimes accompany and manifest interior wounds, produced in the simple and immaterial soul, by the powerful, mystical action of infused love."[21] If twenty-first century-Christians bind their hearts to the sacred heart of the Crucified One, what stigmata will appear as manifestation of infused love?

Catholic theologian Karl Rahner saw devotion to the sacred heart as including a willingness to suffer in pursuing "Christ's law of life."[22] He identified a theology of the sacred heart of Jesus hinging on the idea of reparation, "sharing in the redemptive love of Christ for the world."[23] If we are called to follow this Jesus, surely we must look to all those places where structures and systems give rise to the crucified people, and we must be willing to take on the weight of the world to share their burden. The sacred heart of Jesus calls us to have the heart of Christ, bearing the weight of the tortured in our own being. If our love is to be redemptive, reparation will be the stigmata of infused love.

"LAMB OF GOD,
YOU TAKE AWAY THE SIN OF THE WORLD"

The simultaneity of justice and mercy hears Christians cry out liturgically, "Lamb of God, you take away the sin of the world, have mercy on us." The twin elements of God's judgment and forgiveness, of God's justice and mercy, are held together as we Christians pattern ourselves on the great wisdom teacher of love and hold ourselves accountable for our failures, but see in Jesus the one who takes away the sin of the world. Originally expressed in the Gospel according to John, Jesus as lamb of God is

---

[21] Merton, *What Are These Wounds?*, 126.

[22] Karl Rahner, "Some Theses for a Theology of Devotion to the Sacred Heart," in *The Theology of the Spiritual Life,* vol. 3 in *Theological Investigations* (New York: Crossroad, 1982), 350.

[23] Ibid., 338–40.

identified with the suffering servant of the prophet Isaiah and the Jewish practice of sacrificing a lamb at Passover in remembrance of God's saving action that led people out of their enslavement. The earliest Christians affirmed that Jesus's role is not toward discrete transgressions (of sins), but transforms the condition of the world as a condition of sin.[24] In a twenty-first century world so different from the one in which these liturgical expressions emerged, what might it mean to identify Jesus Christ as one who takes away the sin of the world?

In *Theology for a Social Gospel,* written in the early part of the twentieth century under the exploitative conditions of industrialization in New York City, Walter Rauschenbusch interpreted the ancient notion that Jesus took on the sin of the world by enumerating the social sins that created the conditions for Jesus's death: "As Christian[s] we believe that the death of our Lord concerns us all. Our sins caused it. He bore the sin of the world. . . . How did Jesus bear sins which he did not commit? . . . By his human life Jesus was bound up backward and forward and sideward with the life of humanity."[25] In unparalleled solidarity, Jesus was bound up with humanity in its historical reality, pervaded by sin. Rauschenbusch continues:

> Now this race of ours is pervaded by sin; not only by sporadic acts of folly, waywardness, vice or crime which springs spontaneously from human life, but by organized forces and institutions of evil which have stabilized the power of sin and made it effective. Our analysis of race sin culminated in the recognition of a Kingdom of evil (Chapter IX). Jesus lived in the midst of that Kingdom, and it was this which killed him.[26]

---

[24] See Sandra M. Schneiders, "The Lamb of God and the Forgiveness of Sin(s) in the Fourth Gospel," *Catholic Biblical Quarterly* 73 (2011): 1–29.

[25] Walter Rauschenbusch, *A Theology for the Social Gospel (1917)* (Lousiville, KY: Westminster John Knox Press, 1997), 244–45.

[26] Ibid., 246.

While Rasuchenbusch did not have in view institutionalized racism (he uses *race* in the sense of the *human race*), we might apply his hermeneutic to our own time. Jesus lived in the midst of a kingdom of structural evil, and insofar as we contribute to the evil of institutions, we contribute to the forces that are death-dealing. As Rauschenbush reflects, "[Jesus] did in a very real sense bear the weight of public sins of organized society, and they in turn are causally connected with all private sins."[27]

But the private and institutionalized sins of humanity did not come together only in the first century to bring about the death of the Crucified One through the solidarity of humanity; the sins of the present, our sins, are also linked to this ancient event. In Rauschenbusch's words:

> By repeating the sins of the past we are involved in the guilt of the past. We are linked in a solidarity of evil and guilt with all who have done the same before us, and all who will do the same after us. In so far then as we, by our conscious actions or our passive consent, have repeated the sins which killed Jesus, we have made ourselves guilty of his death. If those who actually killed him stood before us, we could not wholly condemn them, but would have to range ourselves with them as men of their own kind.[28]

Rauschenbusch portrays Jesus as a nonviolent resister to these deadly sins through an intimate identification with the creative love of God. Jesus's God-consciousness is for Rauschenbusch the transformative force that takes away the sin of the world. When humanity learns to understand and to love God in the manner of Jesus Christ, and when God is realized in the world by witnessing God's own life of loving-kindness and forgiveness appropriated by human beings, God and humanity "would enter into spiritual solidarity, and this would be the only effective reconciliation."[29]

---

[27] Ibid., 247.
[28] Ibid., 259.
[29] Ibid., 265.

The Crucified One takes away the sin of the world, illuminating its existence in the structures of our world and enabling their transformation. "In this change of relations [between humanity and God] Christ would be the initiator. His obedience would be the germinal cell from which the new organism would grow. His place within it would be unique. But his aim and effort would be to make himself not unique, but to become, 'the first-born among many brethren.'"[30] In contemplating the Crucified One, we are invited to contemplate our own responsibility for the sins which crucify, but we are also invited to contemplate the love of enemy that Jesus demonstrates in the Gospel telling of his final words: "Forgive them; for they do not know what they are doing" (Luke 23:34). Here is the culmination of the love that Jesus preached and the love Christians are called to follow. As Rauschenbush concludes, Jesus's death "underscored all that he said on love. It put the red seal of sincerity in his words. 'Greater love hath no man than that he give his life for his friends.' Unless he gives it for his enemies too."[31]

If Jesus takes away the sin of the world by illuminating sinful realities and condemning them with his judgment, the transformation of those sinful structures will come through rebalancing the weight of the world. Justice comes in the illuminating of sinful realities, judging them in condemnation, and transforming them. Those who call themselves Christian are to follow his life-giving, death-defying pattern in the practice of love in their own lives: love that does not seek for the self but pursues the reign of God in justice. As Ellacuría writes, "Jesus' death is not the end of the meaning of his life, but rather the end of that pattern that must be repeated and followed in new lives with the hope of resurrection and thereby the seal of exaltation."[32] The Crucified One should stand as haunting presence illuminating the places where Christian practices of transformation must be enacted.

---

[30] Ibid., 265.

[31] Ibid., 271.

[32] Ellacuría, "The Crucified People: An Essay in Historical Soteriology," 207.

THE COLOR OF THE CHRIST

If Christians are to be moved by the cross and pierced like the sacred heart of Jesus, not only their theologies but their iconographies must change. In my own Catholic tradition, sacred art communicates powerfully motivations and moods through symbolism that infuses the place where we gather to remember Jesus Christ. Not only do we hear the stories of Jesus in the proclamation of scripture and remember the ministry and death of Christ in the eucharistic meal, but these ritual forms are situated in sanctuary spaces that are saturated with symbols from the tradition. Enter almost any Catholic church and before you hear the word or eat the bread, you have already encountered the commitments of the community in its stained glass, its statuary, and the symbolic presence of its story in art. Central in this artful communication is the altar space, which is the focus of the ritual expression and the ritual meal, and adorned in so many Catholic altar spaces with representations of the Crucified One.

The Crucified One hovers as an embodied presence over the gathering of the community. He hangs from a cross, a symbol of state-sanctioned torture, haunting those who claim to be formed in his image. Here in the communal gathering, week after week, Catholics are visited artfully by the specter of their God, crucified and raised among them. This specter has the capacity to allow the bodies of those weighted by the oppressions of the world to come to expression. Christ on the cross is not only Jesus of Nazareth but reflects back to us the crimson thread that runs through all history by which power crucifies as it crams, crowds, and concentrates bodies, extinguishing the life within them. The haunting presence of the Crucified One reveals the concentrated bodies of the crucified people, who are a "haunting presence . . . anonymous and exponential,"[33] that might be given expression in the Crucified One. The expression of concentrated bodies,

---

[33] Jean-Luc Nancy, *Corpus*, trans. Richard A. Rand (New York: Fordham University Press, 2008), 79.

however, has a transformative potential that might be the presence of the Divine in the crucified. Taylor writes:

> Concentrated bodies are a perpetually suppurating wound, where bodies and beings are compressed. And yet, there is from the wound a transformative action that at least points, however desperately, to world amid "unworld." It is also a way of communicating. Key to any such transformative impact is a gesture's or action's capacity to haunt, to unsettle those concentrations of power and knowledge where weight is amassed, where injustices as the indistinction and extinction of bodies occurs through breaking, crushing, and stifling.[34]

The Crucified One makes present in the sanctuary space the perpetual wound of the concentrated bodies of the crucified people. The cross reflects back to those gathered the extinction of bodies that runs through history. Its purpose is to unsettle. It demands a response.

Key to the transformative impact of the cross is its capacity to haunt, "to unsettle those concentrations of power and knowledge where weight is amassed," as Taylor puts it. If we have seen that, in the context of the United States, Whiteness is a site of weightlessness and the weight of the world is shifted onto people of color, then when the Crucified One is imaged as White, has the cross lost its transformative power to haunt and unsettle White supremacy? In his study of White Christians and their response to the narratives of Christ's suffering, Clive Marsh suggests that the widespread experience has not been one of collective suffering and that this has repercussions for White Christian ability to identify with the Crucified One. Marsh concludes: "White Christians unwittingly reveal the extent to which their history (personal and collective) cannot adequately identify with the

---

[34] Mark Lewis Taylor, *The Theological and the Political: On the Weight of the World* (Minnneapolis: Fortress Press 2011), 44. Here, Taylor drawing on Nancy, *Corpus*, 47.

crucified figure."[35] While Whiteness does not align with collective suffering, the suffering Christ continues to be imaged as White.

The image of Christ as White was part of the cultural production of a White Christian nation. In their analysis of a late-nineteenth-century illustrated "biography" of Jesus, Henry Ward Beecher's *The Life of Jesus, the Christ* (1871), Blum and Harvey write: "With text and image, Beecher set up Jesus so that white Americans and Europeans could claim him rhetorically as a universal, nonwhite savior but visually as one of their own."[36] That is, the narrative of Christ presents him as the universal human, but the images present him with the characteristics of Whiteness. "Read together, the pictures and the text showed Beecher taking racial particularity (whiteness), wrapping it in religious particularity (Protestant Christianity), and claiming it as human universality."[37]

White Christian churches in America reflect the same visual argument that Beecher presented in his book. The proclamation of Christ as universal model of humanity, when joined with the representation of Jesus in White form, visually aligns Christ with Whiteness. When a White Christ stands in the sanctuary as model of universal humanity, is White supremacy upheld in our liturgical space? As J. S. Siker notes, "The history of Western Christian theology (often articulated in art) has seen the ascendancy of Jesus as a white Christ with a resultant de facto white God endorsing white power claims over other racial/ethnic groups."[38]

---

[35] Clive Marsh, "Black Christs in White Christian Perspective: Some Critical Reflections," *Black Theology* 2, no. 1 (2004): 51.

[36] Edward J. Blum and Paul Harvey, *The Color of Christ: The Son of God and the Saga of Race in America* (Chapel Hill: University of North Carolina Press, 2012), 138–39.

[37] Ibid., 139, referencing Henry Ward Beecher, *The Life of Jesus, the Christ* (New York: J. B. Ford, 1871), 134–37.

[38] J. S. Siker, "Historicizing a Racialized Jesus: Case Studies in the 'Black Christ,' the 'Mestizo Christ,' and White Critique," *Biblical Interpretation* 15 (2007): 27. See also Josiah Ulysses Young, "'Is the White Christ, Too, Distraught by These Dark Sins His Father Wrought?': Dietrich Bonhoeffer and the Problem of the White Christ," *Perspectives In Religious Studies* (Fall 1999), 317–30.

While Christ has been iconographically aligned with Whiteness, the White Christ makes no logical sense in a weighted world where it is Black and Brown and Asian and Arab bodies that are disproportionately among the concentrated and extinguished. If the Crucified One is to make present the crucified people and reflect back to us the crimson thread that runs through history, does it not make more sense to color the Christ so that this ghostly grace might truly unsettle White supremacy?

This is why the image of the White Jesus does us no good: it makes no sense. Whiteness has been the cause of crucifixion, not its target. The social sin of racism requires that the color of the Christ magnifies this injustice and reflects it back to us in the worshiping community so that we might see the sins of White supremacy and racism that continue to crucify. By coloring the Christ, Christians stand at the foot of the cross indicted for the ways that White supremacy has crucified others. So seeing, we might cry out these words: *Lamb of God, who takes away the sin of racism, have mercy on those of us who have benefited from White supremacy, and in taking on the sin of racism and White supremacy, transform us to racial justice that might grant us peace in our world.*

When the Lamb of God takes away the sinful structures of the world and by his judgment reallocates the goodness of creation, those of us who have benefited from the injustice of White supremacy will have already received our reward and will need to ask for God's mercy. Lamb of God, you take away the sin of the world, have mercy on us.

Instead of the White Christ raised high in White churches, the color of the Christ should remind us of race hatred and the costs of our sinfulness. Instead of the sanitized savior tortured without agony, the Crucified One might bear the marks of our inhumanity. Such a Christ image was revelation to the world in the actions of a grieving mother, whose only son was brutally dehumanized, tortured and executed by the power of White supremacy. When two Mississippi men kidnapped, tortured, and executed Emmett Till, his body magnified the social sin of racism. His mother, Mamie Till Bradley, received his broken and bloodied body by train in Chicago. Refusing the direction of the coroner to maintain the closure of the casket, Till Bradley insisted on gazing lovingly on her son's corpse to take in the specificity and intimacy of the horror as real and irreversible.

> "Darling, you have not died in vain," she said to Emmett, as she "looked at that horribly mangled monstrosity"; "your life has been sacrificed for something."[39]

Instead of closing in on her grief, Till Bradley insisted further on the public viewing of an open casket and the publication of Emmett's horrific disfigurement in the national press. *This is my body.* James Cone writes:

> Six hundred thousand people viewed his bruised body and attended the funeral, and many millions more saw the *Jet* magazine photos [September 1955] that traveled around the world. "This is not for Emmett," Mrs. Bradley said, "because my boy can't be helped now, but to make it safe for other boys. Unless an example is made of the lynchers of Emmett, it won't be safe for a Negro to walk the streets anywhere in America."[40]

The torture and death of Emmett Till enabled his mother to hear the voice of the resurrected Jesus speak "of hope that, although white racists could take her son's life, they could not deprive his life and death of an ultimate meaning. As in the resurrection of the Crucified One, God could transmute defeat into triumph, ugliness into beauty, despair into hope, the cross into resurrection."[41] In the haunting of Emmett Till we hear Christ's

---

[39] Cone, *The Cross and the Lynching Tree*, 67. Cone is referencing Christopher Metress, ed., *The Lynching of Emmett Till* (Charlottesville: University of Virginia Press, 2002), 21–32.

[40] Ibid., 67, again citing Metress.

[41] Ibid., 69.

words: "This is my body, given up for you." Mamie Till gave over her crucified son, and the world would be haunted by the Crucified One and empowered into the transformation of the civil rights decade that followed, as Rosa Parks, Medgar Evers, James Cone, and countless other leaders would be emboldened by the horror of Emmett's death and the humanity that was his life.

Who, today, must be raised in the specter of the Crucified One for the transformation of the world? Womanist theologian Kelly Brown Douglas raises the specter of another crucified son, Trayvon Martin, in a theology that challenges the stand-your-ground culture of White supremacy. In the image that adorns her book, the 2013 lithograph by Margo Humphrey entitled "Fear Not! I Got You," the pieta of Mary cradling the broken body taken down from the cross is rendered as the Virgin with her son in a hoodie holding a pack of Skittles. In theology and image the Crucified One illuminates the social sin of racism that takes the lives of Black bodies at an astounding rate. The bodies of families broken by eviction[42] or young people concentrated into overcrowded, underfunded schools[43] might be haunting images that bring Christ's judgment upon us for the social sins that continue to be disproportionately death-dealing for people of color. Latino farmworkers—who work so that Americans might have the food to live—make up "approximately one half of US farmworkers,"

---

[42] See Matthew Desmond, *Policy Research Brief*, MacArthur Foundation (March 2014), https://www.macfound.org. "Those evicted are disproportionately women from black and Hispanic neighborhoods. . . . In high-poverty black neighborhoods, one male renter in 33 and one woman in 17 is evicted. In high-poverty white neighborhoods, in contrast, the ratio is 134:1 for men and 150:1 for women. Women from black neighborhoods represented only 9.6 percent of the population, but they accounted for 30 percent of the evictions in Milwaukee."

[43] Race Forward: The Center for Racial Justice Innovation, "New Report Outlines Impact of Racial Profiling in US Public Schools" (October 30, 2001). The report, "Racial Profiling and Punishment in US Public Schools," states: "At the national level, schools with a majority of students of color are 3.7 times more likely to be severely overcrowded than schools with less than 5 percent students of color."

an occupation that in 2011 had a fatality rate "seven times higher than the fatality rate for all workers in private industry."[44] This might haunt us as the crucified presence, allowing us to hear anew the words of an ancient Christian community: "Listen! The wages of the laborers who mowed your fields, which you kept back by fraud, cry out, and the cries of the harvesters have reached the ears of the Lord of hosts" (James 5:4).

In another specter of the Crucified One, the faces of three young Muslims executed in a White Christian nation that manufactures hate of our Muslim neighbors might be Christ's judgment upon us. An artist's rendering of the tortured prisoners at Guantanamo Bay along the stations of the cross is yet another symbol of the crucified one(s) who might be a haunting presence in our worship space. In raising the crucified one(s), White Christians might hear with new ears the call of the earliest communities. With images of global refugees we might hear once again: "The alien who resides with you shall be to you as the citizen among you; you shall love the alien as yourself, for you were aliens in the land of Egypt: I am the Lord your God" (Lev 19:34).

An antiracist, anti-supremacist Christology is not only a thought experiment. The earliest Christians didn't just tell their stories; they aimed to use Jesus's life story as one that would shape their own lives. Telling and hearing the story motivated them to action, so that they could say, "It is no longer I who live, but it is Christ who lives in me" (Gal 2:20). Liturgically and in letters they reminded one another:

> Be doers of the word, and not merely hearers who deceive themselves. For if any are hearers of the word and not doers, they are like those who look at themselves in a mirror; for they look at themselves and, on going away, immediately forget what they were like. But those who look into the perfect law, the law of liberty, and persevere, being not

---

[44] United States Department of Labor, OSHA, "Safety and Health Topics: Agricultural Operations" (Washington DC).

hearers who forget but doers who act—they will be blessed
in their doing. (James 1:22–25)

Instead of looking in a mirror and forgetting who we are, the
gaze fixed upon the Crucified One insists that we be doers of the
word of love enacted in a weighted world.

Like the early Christians we might be realists as well. Our
ancient forbears saw clearly the limits of our human lives and the
short span of earthly existence we actually have allotted to us.
Realistically, the author of an early letter reminded his readers:
"What is your life? For you are a mist that appears for a little
while and then vanishes" (James 4:14). But in this fleeting existence, in the short time allotted to us, embedded in the mystery
of existence and enveloped in the mystery of love, Christians
from ancient times to today have affirmed a meaningfulness to
that "little while" in Jesus's pattern of love. We might join them
in crafting a meaningful existence as beings-toward-death, who
participate in the mystery of life and love in the way of Jesus and
the way of the cross. How are we to love in a weighted world?
We next take up that question and the possibilities of action that
might continue the Christian cloud of witnesses for the twenty-
first century.

6

CHRISTIAN LOVE
IN A WEIGHTED WORLD

THE STORY OF THE CHRISTIAN tradition might be conceived as a love story: a narrative that identifies love at the heart of reality but recognizes the deep challenges that love is for human beings. The history of modern Christianity, however, has been of an epic failure to love, where the stories of Christian tradition were mobilized for the self-love of White supremacy and the destruction of non-White, non-Christian others. As the preceding chapter argued, we need the renewed resource of symbolic capital to envision Christ as model of Christian love in a weighted world. Unlike the way Christ has functioned for the dispossession of non-White, non-Christian others, this Christ expresses God's love as judgment for Christians in the haunting presence of the crucified. The Crucified One made present in liturgical space indicts Christians for the way they have contributed to the disfigurement and torture of those upon whom they have shifted the weight of the world. This judgment is a necessary first step for Christians who recall the emphasis we find in the Gospel of Matthew where Jesus called for the repentance of sins and the judgment of fruits: "Every tree therefore that does not bear good fruit is cut down and thrown into the fire" (Matt 3:10). In the haunting presence of the Crucified One, we stand judged.

But as we saw in Chapter 4, judgment is a crucial but not solitary element of the kind of love the Gospels recount. In addition to judgment there are emphases also on healing, intimacy, and love of enemy. Focused on the embodiment of this love in the Crucified One, Christians must mobilize love in a new way to redistribute the weight of the world through judgment, intimacy, love of enemy, and healing. This takes theological reimagining and practical action. The theological reimagining that was the focus of the preceding chapter illuminated the symbol of Christ as a haunting presence reminding Christians of all those places where *we* are the crucifiers, where our theologies of supremacy underwrite legislation that secures well-being for some and not others. Theologically, we are called to hear the haunting of our neighbors of color and our neighbors of all faiths, and to enact the Christian call to love across borders and boundaries. If we revisit the multidimensional portrayal of love from the New Testament accounts, might we imagine ways for love to be enacted through practical action in our weighted world?

The gospel portraits of Christian love holds a multiplicity of dimensions. In John's Gospel, Jesus illumines the need for intimate love among lifelong communities of mutual care that culminates in laying down one's life for one's friend. But the pattern we envisioned includes expanding our circle of those whom we call friends. In the Gospel of Mark, not only one's friends but strangers receive Jesus's love as healing. This outpouring of love, however, comes with critical vision and with judgment, as the emphases in Matthew's Gospel seem to sound most clearly. And Luke's Gospel extends these concentric circles from intimacy to stranger to the radical love of enemy. As New Testament scholar Aaron J. Kuecker argues, the central characteristics of Jesus in this Gospel are "enemy love and radical generosity."[1] These are qualities that enable those who follow him

---

[1] Aaron Kuecker, "'You Will Be Children of the Most High': An Inquiry into Luke's Narrative Account of Theosis," *Journal of Theological Interpretation* 8, no. 2 (2014): 215.

to share in Jesus's God-likeness. Through patterning ourselves on Jesus's love in the form of intimacy, healing, judgment, and love of enemy, we too share in God-likeness. In the words of an ancient Christian community, "if we love one another, God lives in us" (1 John 4:12).

The foregoing exploration of this book reminds us that this love is not easy and that it is not done in the twenty-first century without the weight of the preceding centuries of Christians' epic failures to love forming the landscape of our loving. The question remains, how do we love in a weighted world? In the stories that follow I illuminate examples of loving in the various modes identified in the Gospels and describe these practices as Christian practices of love in a weighted world. Through considering Christian practices as they have been embodied by everyday Christians, we might vision the cloud of witnesses or the communion of everyday saints who have had the courage to love. Hearing their stories might be a study in the point of being Christian—in finding the meaning of life in love, a love that includes judgment, intimacy, healing, and love of enemy. These practices of everyday Christians, insofar as we are able to follow them, might also be the manifestation of *our* love in a weighted world. The project of love in a weighted world is an ongoing one. What follows is not a comprehensive plan but just a few among the many steps that might be taken in an orientation that aims to follow the pattern of love from the Gospels. They help us to see the point and purpose of Christian wisdom as it manifests not only in antiquity but in lives of meaning and purpose today. Returning to the categories and practices we unearthed in the study of early Christian sources, we might ask whether an ancient wisdom might help us to love in our weighted world.

PREACHING CHRIST CRUCIFIED: THE INDICTMENT OF THE CROSS IN LOVE'S JUDGMENT

Christians have been responsible not only for the material conditions enacted through historical decisions and legislation, but also for theologies and ideologies that prioritize Christians and host a sliding scale of humanity that privileges Whiteness and envisions Christ as White. As the close of Chapter 3 suggested, Christians need to be held responsible for the symbolic capital they manufacture and mobilize, allowing the well-being of people of color and the well-being of all crucified people to be the guiding methodological principle. As a project of symbolic capital by which values are articulated and enacted, Christian theology and Christian preaching must hold dispossessed others clearly in view.

The insistence on holding the dispossessed other as *the* criterion in Christian faith and practice brings us back to the essential story of Christian love in a new way. Love looks like Christ crucified—tortured and hanging from a cross. Expressing a love that would tolerate no boundaries, no limits to human well-being, his love is witnessed in a willingness to die as a result of this boundary-challenging way of being. This is the heart of the gospel message: the creative force at the heart of creation loves across all boundaries, and faithfulness to this vision of love to the end is possible.[2] But the witness of Christ crucified is also affirmation of the tragedy of the cross as the negative measure of where human love has failed. The failure to love is the indictment of the cross. In light of the historical dispossession of people of color and people of other faiths, the judgment of love must be upon the supremacist theo-logic that has been enacted in Jesus's name.

Among the stories Jesus tells is the story of judgment unheeded. A rich man, finding himself dead and in the torment of hell, begs that the dispossessed Lazarus be allowed to return from the dead as a sign and warning to the man's brothers so that they might change their ways. The rich man is told that Moses and the prophets already have warned humanity of this judgment and the need for love. "If they do not listen to Moses and the prophets, neither will they be convinced even if someone rises from the dead" (Luke 16:31). The judgment Jesus announces is nothing new. The heart of Torah in loving God and neighbor is warning

---

[2] For this way of framing the good news of the Gospels, see Jon Sobrino, *Christ the Liberator* (Maryknoll, NY: Orbis Books, 2001), 217.

and judgment, as is the call of compassion from the teaching of the Buddha, the straight path in the wisdom of the Qur'an, the recognition of divinity resident in the other in Hinduism, and the turn to our fellow human beings at the heart of humanism. The wisdom of love and compassion is not new. People of all faiths and varying convictions have heard the warning call of love. Christ is not unique in his message of love, but Christ crucified is the uniquely Christian sign and witness to where we are indicted by our failures and emboldened in the logic of love at all costs.

One point of participating in a wisdom tradition is that the tools the tradition has offered provide resources for our living. The stories of Jesus told and retold in the ancient world provided keys to understanding the human condition and what it meant to be a person in the world, a person in face of the mystery of God, and a person in relationship. Participating in a wisdom tradition opens us to the practices of the many who have gone before and asks whether they might be useful for us today. Resources for living come from surprising places. While they often must be translated into terms that resonate with our context because they come from out of contexts very different from our own, they might still offer material for our self-understanding and for our growth.

It is a Christian raised in medieval traditions who offers us the practical step of contemplating the judgment rendered by the Crucified One. Ignatius of Loyola's approach to sin and his prescientific worldview may be different from our own, but nevertheless he might bridge the practice of indictment with transformation. Ignatius is a classic figure of transformation. He came from a family of prestige and a position of military power. When he was recovering from the violence of a battle that disfigured his leg as a young man, Ignatius began a lifelong contemplation on the question: Who am I called to become? The answers he found, after years of contemplation and searching, he wrote into a manual for others to undertake the same process of discernment and self-understanding. In his *Spiritual Exercises* seekers are invited into four weeks of contemplation. Through reflection on the person of Jesus, week one calls to mind one's failings; week two is an invitation to consider Jesus's life and work; week three is a contemplation of the drama of Jesus's death; and week four considers living in the joy of the resurrection. In the movement of the four weeks of the *Exercises,* seekers embed themselves in the Christian narrative and are offered the opportunity for the story to shape their life.[3]

It is in the first week's contemplation of sin that love as judgment is most clearly in view. If the world is an expression of God's creative love, and we are called to love God through love of neighbor, the contemplation of our failing is a crucial step in the Christian life. In the colloquy that closes the first exercise of the first week, we are drawn to the foot of the cross. Ignatius writes:

> Imagine Christ our Lord suspended on the cross before you, and converse with him in a colloquy: How is it that he, although he is the Creator, has come to make himself a human being? How is it that he has passed from eternal life to death here in time, and to die in this way for my sins?
>
> In a similar way, reflect on yourself and ask: What have I done for Christ? What am I doing for Christ? What ought I do for Christ?[4]

Contemplation on the cross of Christ was essential to the spiritual growth Ignatius envisioned; he closed this contemplation with a meditation on the Lord's Prayer.[5]

Joining the cloud of witnesses and the communion of saints, Christians join themselves to those like Dorothy Day in contemplating the purpose of creation and our failures to fulfill it. Many remember Day as an advocate for the dispossessed. She founded

---

[3] See Roger Haight, *Christian Spirituality for Seekers: Reflections on the Spiritual Exercises of Ignatius Loyola* (Maryknoll, NY: Orbis Books, 2012).

[4] *The Spiritual Exercises of Saint Ignatius,* trans. and commentary George E. Ganss (Chicago: Loyola Press, 1992), 42.

[5] For a meditation on the Lord's Prayer, see Chapter 4.

the Catholic Worker to form community and feed those who were in need. She was also a tireless advocate for those crushed by the weight of the world in her journalism, which unearthed everyday, structural injustices of the economic order. Despite a life spent in service to and communion with others, Day herself experienced the limits of love. For Day, self-examination was a painful study because of the way we turn too easily to our own self-love and self-protection and forget that the love that emanates from the center of the universe is a love destined to turn outward. It was never meant for the individual alone but for the entirety of existence in the well-being of all creation and all created realities. Day placed herself in the cloud of witnesses as she quoted Thomas Merton and his drawing on poet William Blake to affirm: "We are put on earth for a little space that we may learn to bear the beams of love"[6] Stretching back not only through the foundational Christian communities but our Jewish brothers and sisters before us, we are reminded in theology and poetry of the essential witness of love: love God, love your neighbor as yourself. But enacting this love and bearing the "beams of love" are not easy. Even Day had to pray, "Take away my heart of stone and give me a heart of flesh."[7]

The symbol set of the Christian tradition, centered on the life, person, death, and resurrection of Jesus, provides an orientation to the world that asks about the limitations we put on love and invites us always and again to love. The Crucified One and the crucified people serve as the criteria on which to judge the successes and failures of our love. From a lifelong commitment to shifting the weight of the world Dorothy Day reflected, "My whole life, so far, my whole experience has been that our failure has been not to love enough."[8] If our failure as a human

---

[6] William Blake, "The Little Black Boy," quoted in Doublas V. Steere's "Foreword" to Thomas Merton, *Contemplative Prayer* (1969; reissue, New York: Image Classics, 1971), xv.

[7] Dorothy Day, *Selected Writings,* ed. Robert Ellsberg (Maryknoll, NY: Orbis Books, 1982), 181.

[8] Dorothy Day, *On Pilgrimage* (1948), in Day, *Selected Writings,* 220.

community has been the failure of not loving enough, as evidenced in the disequilibrium and imbalance of a weighted world, then the Crucified One and the crucified people still function as the assessment and indictment of the efficacy of Christian wisdom. In the words of Martin Luther King, Jr., "Everywhere and at all times, the love ethic of Jesus is a radiant light revealing the ugliness of our stale conformity."[9]

The project of this book has suggested that the wisdom of Christian tradition is wisdom about love. I've suggested that this love might provide tools for meaningful lives in the face of the mystery of our existence and that Christian tradition might still speak to us today and might help us undo the sin of White supremacy. But, like Jesus's critique of religious supremacies of his day, we might be reminded of the ever-present temptation to give in to another set of desires: the desires of symbolic capital that promise us (as they did Jesus in the desert) the rewards of glory, honor, credit, praise, and fame. The constant pull of these desires is a consistent feature of human existence, found also within Christian communities. King explains: "Gradually, however, the church became so entrenched in wealth and prestige that it began to dilute the strong demands of the Gospel and to conform to the ways of the world. And ever since the church has been a weak and ineffectual trumpet making uncertain sounds."[10] The argument of this book, an argument King also laid out, is that a return to the fundamentals of love might renew not only the world but Christian communities themselves.

With Ignatius of Loyola as a guide to putting love into practice, a renewed church might gather in self-examination. If, through historical choices and legislation, White Christians have created the conditions of dispossession for our Black, Latino, and Native American neighbors, this church might ask: What have we done to the crucified? If White Christians continue to

---

[9] Martin Luther King, Jr., "Transformed Nonconformist," in *Strength to Love: Martin Luther King, Jr.,* foreword Coretta Scott King (Minneapolis: Fortress Press, 2010), 13.

[10] Ibid., 16.

ignore the dispossessions and make future decisions with White priorities in view, this church might ask: What are we doing to the crucified? If we can see clearly the history of dispossession, the continued impact of disequilibrium, and the responsibility we have for shifting the weight of the world, this church might ask: What ought we do for the crucified? While Ignatius's *Spiritual Exercises* provide the personalized approach of self-examination, we need also to broaden this to the communal dimension of our gathering community. How might this self-examination be preached so that love is fostered through the necessary first step of judgment in the setting of Christian communities committed to enacting love in a weighted world?

The private housekeeping of self-examination is an important project for Christians pursuing the self-judgment that love requires. But self-examination, while important, necessarily lends itself to reproducing privilege through the blind spots we inhabit. A crucial component of our growth and understanding is the recognition of the limits of our view.[11] Through honest dialogue and interfaith encounter we open ourselves up to the ongoing crucifixions that we participate in, not as we imagine them but as the others experience them. The *listening* required of White Christians in antiracist practice and interreligious dialogue is a crucial component in the lines of love in a weighted world. The point of interracial and interreligious dialogue is not to prove *our* point, but to hear the haunting of those on whom the weight of the world has been shifted by our Christian claims and Christian practices.

BUILDING INTIMACY AS A RESPONSE TO THE INDICTMENT OF THE CRUCIFIED ONE

If Christian congregations are to help us in our learning how to love, and if this love is aimed at undoing religio-racial divisions

---

[11] For a discussion of the four avenues by which bias occurs, see *Insight: A Study of Human Understanding*, vol. 3, in *Collected Works of Bernard Lonergan*, ed. Frederick E. Crowe and Robert Doran (Toronto: University of Toronto Press, 1997), 214–20.

and dispossessions, the intimate community where we learn to love must be multi-racial. The problem is, of course, that the most intimate spaces where Christians learn to love in community have also been compromised by the historical choices of Christians in the past. In light of the refusal of White Christians in the past to share worship and power within Christian congregations, too many Christian communities remain mono-racial and segregated. With this landscape in view, we hear Jesus's call captured in the Gospel according to John in a new way: "Love one another as I have loved you." The form of this love is intimacy.

If the space in which Christians learn to love is the space of intimacy within the church, we must hear again the words of Martin Luther King, Jr., who looked out on our landscape and said, "We must face the sad fact that at eleven o'clock on Sunday morning when we stand to sing, 'In Christ there is no East or West,' we stand in the most segregated hour of America."[12] If we are Christian seekers, does the congregation in which we learn to love reflect the multi-racial reality of our American context? If we are seekers asking after the possibilities of love in a weighted world, are there multi-racial congregations available that could be our community of practice for learning Christian love? Sadly, too many of us must answer no to these questions. As scholar, pastor, and antiracism trainer Joseph Barndt has expressed it:

> It is difficult to imagine a greater contradiction than that the Christian church, called by God to be a messenger of freedom and liberation, is itself in bondage to racism and virtually powerless to preach its own most central truth. . . . We are still a deeply divided people of God unable to represent a racially unified body of Christ.[13]

---

[12] Martin Luther King, Jr., "Remaining Awake through a Great Revolution," sermon delivered at the National Cathedral, Washington DC, March 31, 1968.

[13] Joseph Barndt, *Becoming an Anti-Racist Church: Journeying toward Wholeness* (Minneapolis: Fortress Press, 2011), 104, 108.

How are we shaped in the Christian call to love as intimacy in such a way that it actually serves racist purposes of segregation rather than the antiracist purposes our world needs?

The practice to follow here is what many congregations have attempted in the last twenty years: the commitment to becoming an antiracist church. As Barndt describes, this is a project and a process that has emerged from the civil rights era and US attention to multiculturalism. But the Christian church in America still has a long way to go to become a truly multicultural, antiracist institution. Barndt not only describes the process undertaken by many Christian congregations, but he also provides resources and tools for congregations interested in pursuing this Christian call. In *Becoming an Anti-Racist Church* he provides both the history of Christian churches in America as a White Christian nation *and* materials for undertaking the project of moving one's own congregation from its racist history toward an antiracist future. Enacting love as intimacy for healing our world requires that Christian congregations commit themselves to this task of interracial renewal as antiracist, transformed, and transforming institutions.

Just as Christian churches must heal the divide created by America's White supremacist racial project, they must simultaneously undertake to heal the divisions caused by a logic of identity that rests on Christian supremacy. Here, the ritual encounter with people of other faiths might be an important step as well. In entering the space of religious others at prayer, those who are welcomed experience something of the intimacy of relationship that religious others enjoy with the Divine. In the interfaith movement of working across the lines of different religious traditions, it is this space of ritual—or *inter-riting*—that might enact love as intimacy.

Witnessing the other in prayer helps to destabilize our notions of God and invites us into a more complex, because now holy, relationship with others. In the intimacy of their lives laid bare before God, we might see things in a new way. If the theology I have inherited from a logic of Christian supremacy has asserted that the beliefs and practices of the other are deficient in comparison with my Christian beliefs and practices, the counter-affirmation through the practices of the other (namely, beliefs and practices that bring others in touch with the Divine) is an important component to challenge the death-dealing theologies of supremacy. This challenge cannot come from within our own tradition (its logic so tightly bound to Christian supremacy) but must come from an intimate access to the beliefs and practices of the other.

As a further element that begins the healing of a weighted world, the opportunity for inter-riting in the presence of bodies that have been racialized is another form of *listening* we might undertake. Inter-riting may be a necessary step in the repentance required of a White Christian nation, because the rites of the racialized other implicitly insist that neither Whiteness nor Christianity is the arbiter of truth, of goodness, or of religiosity. In the context of inter-riting the gendered and raced specificity conveys potently the sacred significance of Black and Brown bodies in a way that only reading their sacred texts or learning about their beliefs does not allow. Experiencing the embodiment of the other as a vehicle of divine presence provides an opportunity to counteract the White supremacy that has poisoned Christian practice and has shaped a White Christian nation. That inter-riting is not only interreligious but is interracial communicates profoundly that Black and Brown bodies matter; they are of sacred significance as vehicles for the Divine among us. Those who inhabit Black and Brown bodies surely must know this. But for those of us who have been poisoned by the witchcraft of White supremacy to internalize ideologies of racial superiority and inferiority, embodied access to this theological truth is unimaginably important.

As a practice to follow, the invitation of sharing ritual is one that has been enacted by many in the interfaith movement. The intimacy of lives intertwined with the life of God, even in ways we do not understand, was the experience of my class when we visited a Hindu temple. While Hindus share with Christians, Muslims, and Jews the affirmation of God's reality, Hindu tradition sees God manifest in a multiplicity of forms. God may encounter humanity through the forms of Hinduism's many deities: Sarasvati, Lakshmi, Vishnu, Siva, and so many more. When Hindu practitioners enter the temple, they understand themselves to be in the presence of God in an intimate way; they come to see and be seen by the Divine.

While America has been manufacturing a religio-racial project as a White Christian nation, our neighbors of other faiths have been working also to craft America as a multi-religious, multi-racial nation.[14] So many of our neighbors of other faiths see themselves precisely *as* neighbors and are willing to extend hospitality to others in the interest of interfaith understanding. This was the case when our warm and welcoming host invited our group of non-Hindus to witness darshan, or the ritual through which God is seen, in Queens, New York. While an important experience for interfaith love of neighbor, the incorporation into ritual was also an experience of interfaith intimacy. At my request and donation, the priest dedicated the devotion to Ganesh for the well-being of our group. With twenty-five of us gathered in the altar room, we could witness the embodied approach to God with sights, sounds, smells, tastes, and touch that communicated to us through the body's receptors in a powerful way. Our bodies and senses invited us to participate. Students were neither required nor requested, but when the priest returned from Ganesh with the lamp flame of good blessings, each one of us stepped forward with hands cupped and received, seeing the light, feeling its warmth, breathing in its blessing. Intuitively, out of curiosity, out of respect for the relationship being offered, no single reason can be given for our action. But, to a person, we participated in this Hindu ritual, receiving blessings from the deity, and tangibly receiving a sacred gift in the taking of prasad (ritual food). Relationship was formed out of the sharing of divine-human intimacy, and there was something intimate about being welcomed into

---

[14] For an overview of this development, see Diana Eck, *A New Religious America: How a "Christian Country" Has Become the World's Most Religiously Diverse Nation* (San Francisco: Harper, 2001).

interfaith relation through our bodies, our senses, our selves. We were not just thinking through a comparison of ideas, but we were participating in the Hindu practice of encountering God, of loving God. There was something contagious in this love of God that we experienced as the love of *us* as neighbor when the priest brought to us the blessing. It was as if we were wrapped up in the love that flowed between God and neighbor and could not refuse the invitation to be in relationship.

In the interracial and interreligious context of shared worship, an intimacy is allowed to develop. The close religious and racial intimacy of shared worship might give witness to a relationship, however brief, that fosters the sense that we, neighbors in America, are in this together. It might remind us of our ontological condition of bodies in balance, and as Christians we might hear again our ancient forebears: "No one has ever seen God; if we love one another, God lives in us" (1 John 4:12). The beauty of this form of intimacy as a form of Christian practice for a weighted world is that Christians cannot undertake it alone; it requires love across lines of difference and thus it requires religio-racial others. As a practice of healing divisions in our weighted world, might the love that is fostered through ritual intimacy be a Christian form of the practice of love in our weighted world?

LOVE AS LEGISLATION: THE HEALING OF INTEGRAL SALVATION

Building relationships of intimacy across religious and racial difference, Christian communities might pursue the love as intimacy that we saw was hallmark of the Gospel according to John. But the intimate expression of love must also follow the concentric circles out into the world. And like the world of Mark's Gospel, our world is inhabited by people who are hurting. The people of Jesus's world are bleeding, they are withered, they have seizures and spasms, they are estranged, they are dying, they are dead. At the closing of the Gospel according to Mark the sign of those who believe and will be saved is that when they lay hands on the sick, those who are hurting recover (16:18).

In thinking about Jesus as healer in contemporary perspective, liberation theologians have offered us the vision of Jesus bringing an "integral salvation." They see his healing action as one that embraces the whole person and aims to make persons whole in such a way as to bring them to the fullness of life and integration in community. To heal means to bring persons to the fullness of life as the bishops envisioned at Vatican II: where all experience the well-being of sufficient food, clothing, shelter, the intimacy of family, the right to education, employment, respect, privacy, and religious freedom. We have seen that in the history of America as a White Christian nation and in the demographics of our current landscape, people of color and people of other faiths are regularly denied this fullness of well-being. At this point in our nation's healing, Christians need to make a religio-racial argument to prioritize the well-being of the dispossessed and to bring an integral healing to our world. As Dorothy Day expressed it, "The vision is this. We are working for 'a new heaven and a new *earth*, wherein justice dwelleth.' We are trying to say with action, 'Thy will be done on *earth* as it is in heaven.'"[15] Like other Christians who have drawn from the Gospels a practical vision, Day saw the call of Christian love to be the transformation of the world toward the world that Jesus envisioned as the reign of God. God's will, God's reign, includes the well-being of creation and humanity within it. The sign that we believe and are saved is that healing will come through our hands.

The healing of integral salvation will necessarily need to focus on those structural forms of dispossession that have come through legislation. When we seek to prioritize the dispossessed in legislative reparation, we hear again the call to love in the Gospels, namely, that this work is not easy. Jesus says: "If you want to be followers, take up your cross and follow me" (Matt 16:24). At the same time, we hear the judgment of Matthew's

---

[15] Day, *Selected Writings*, 91.

love and perhaps we are indicted as a whole generation in which "this people's heart has grown dull and their ears are hard of hearing" (13:14). Caught in the web of a weighted world, we seek our own well-being and struggle for the recognition we need for our individual survival. But this is precisely the message of the Gospels—that the love that is needed for healing the world is not easy. "Sell what you own; . . . then come, follow me" (Mark 10:21) Jesus says to those who would be his followers; "those who lose their life for my sake will find it" (Matt 16:25; see also Mark 8:35; John 9:24).

In witnessing to the gospel message in her life and her loves, Sister Simone Campbell calls for twenty-first century Christians to embrace a theology of insecurity.[16] What she means by this is that we have become accustomed to creating the conditions for our own security through a fear that forces us inward, and that we have piled weight onto others for the purpose of our own well-being. To secure the future of *some* children, we pour money into local education that is confined to our communities. To secure the well-being of *some* communities, we have policing practices that produce racialized disparity. To secure well-being within our borders, we act globally both economically and militarily in ways that compromise others' well-being. What Campbell sees is that the struggle for security has the consequence of shifting the weight of the world onto others. But the Christian faith stance ought to be one of trusting that the God who is source of the universe is enough, that human security rests primarily in a fundamental trust in the goodness and sufficiency of the mysterious source of all that is. Campbell invites us to follow Jesus in a renewed way, a way that relinquishes our need for individual security, trusting in the fundamental love at the heart of creation and to seeking to rebalance the weight of the world.

A theology of insecurity realizes that in following the Christian call to love we are putting ourselves in the places of precariousness and risk as a faith practice. Dorothy Day reflected on risk

---

[16] Sister Simone Campbell is the executive director of the social justice lobbying group NETWORK.

in the everyday practices of her context: "Martyrdom is not gallantly standing before a firing squad. Usually it is the losing of a job because of not taking a loyalty oath, or buying a war bond, or paying a tax."[17] What are the everyday practices that involve risk today? What are the strains of the powerful status quo that have lulled us into conformity, with which our Christian call will put us in conflict? As Ellacuría writes, "A Reign of God that does not enter into conflict with a history configured by the power of sin, is not the Reign of God of Jesus, however deeply spiritual it may appear (just as the Reign of God that does not enter into conflict with the malice and evil of personal existence is also not the Reign of God of Jesus)."[18] Christian love is *not* easy, but love as healing the world of injustice *is* the call to Christians. To *all* Christians.

In the words of Dorothy Day, "Too little has been stressed the idea that *all* are called."[19] But all are not called in the same way. Campbell reflects on this by encouraging Christians to consider the particularity of their life circumstances and to recognize that no one will be able to do everything, but that everyone will be able to do something. She echoes the sentiment of Day, who wrote:

> The thing is to recognize that not all are called, not all have the vocation, to demonstrate in this way, to fast, to endure the pain and long-drawn-out-nerve-racking suffering of prison life. We do what we can, and the whole field of all the Works of Mercy is open to us. There is a saying, "Do what you are doing." If you are a student, study, prepare, in order to give to others, and keep alive in yourself the vision of a new social order. All work, whether building, increasing food production, running credit unions, working

---

[17] Dorothy Day, "Inventory," *The Catholic Worker* (January 1951); in Day, *Selected Writings*, 105.

[18] Ignacio Ellacuría, "Theology as the Ideological Moment of Ecclesial Praxis," trans. Anna Bonta Moreland and Kevin F. Burke, in *Ignacio Ellacuría: Essays on History, Liberation, and Salvation*, ed. Michael E. Lee (Maryknoll, NY: Orbis Books, 2013), 269.

[19] Day, *On Pilgrimage*, 216.

in factories which produce for true human needs, working the smallest of industries, the handicrafts—all these things can come under the heading of the Works of Mercy, which are the opposite of the works of war.[20]

If we return to the portrait of our weighted world examined in Chapter 3, we might see more concretely the structural transformation that is the rebalancing of the weight of the world. In our earlier exploration we saw the interrelated systems of wealth, land ownership and home ownership, education, health, and security. We have seen the ways that legislation enacted dispossessions and enhancements that prioritized White citizens in all of these areas, as well as the ways Christian symbolic capital was mobilized in these efforts. If Christians are to enact the healing to which we are called, we must love through legislation that rebalances the weight of the world. These movements are afoot, and Christians might heed the haunting of the Crucified One to join the movement for a living wage, where our economic system working for all, not just for some, is the vision we hold out and work toward. We might enact legislation that enables funding for education to be shared more broadly than the limits of our local community. We might support Native peoples in their struggle for sovereignty, or envision practices for homeownership that would empower the disempowered and bring to reality communities of religious, racial, and economic diversity.[21] Reforms in our police and prison systems would be seen as evidence that we were heeding the call of Christian love in a weighted world.

In addition to addressing legislation that might shift the weight of the world as a Christian practice, attention might also be paid

---

[20] Day, *Selected Writings*, 180.

[21] On this point Richard Rothstein offers very specific plans of action to address "exclusionary zoning laws, placing low- and moderate-income housing in predominantly white suburbs, and ending federal subsidies for communities that fail to reverse policies that led to racial exclusion" (Richard Rothstein, "Why Our Schools Are Segregated," *Educational Leadership: Faces of Poverty* 70, no. 8 (May 2013).

to the ways that local ordinances reflect political decisions that continue to privilege Christian communities and harbor Christian supremacism. One example of this is the resistance many communities have had to building or expanding houses of faith of the varying traditions of the world. Through arguments about parking and building code, or demonstrations of resistance, people of the world's faiths have been denied the right to religious freedom when they are denied access through legislation that supports their worshiping communities. Might Christians find themselves at city council meetings or other demonstrations of support for their neighbors of other faiths as a sign of Christian hospitality and healing in a weighted world?

LOVE OF ENEMY: CHRISTIAN RESPONSIBILITY TO DISMANTLE VALUE-LADEN OPPOSITIONS

Here, we arrive at the foundational necessity of striving for the well-being of our world in ways that challenge the value-laden categories of race and religion that we have constructed. Simone Campbell says that the Christian vision is one for the well-being of the 100 percent. In this, she draws attention to the value-laden oppositions that can be reproduced as we seek our own well-being, or even prioritize the well-being of the dispossessed. She echoes the project of Luke's love of enemy, aligned also with the recognition that at the level of ontology (or being itself) love in a weighted world must have a comprehensive view of the well-being of all. Although it is countercultural and might feel counterintuitive, the call to love of enemy and the dissolution of the value-laden opposition of friend and enemy makes perfect sense for loving in a weighted world. For the weight of the world is precisely a reality that circulates through the global, *ontological* network of our sociality. In our social ontology we are as human beings ultimately and intimately interconnected, and within that interconnected network we struggle for well-being. But if we struggle for our own well-being alone and in the process shift weight onto others, they in turn will struggle, inevitably seeking to shift the weight onto yet another or perhaps back onto us. A social ontology requires that we recognize that we cannot afford to have enemies when our lives, our well-being, and our very being are wrapped up with all those other bodies with whom we share our space. Love of enemy makes perfect sense in a weighted world. But that does not make it easy to do.

To pursue the possibility of love of enemy in a weighted world, I introduce Father Paolo Dall'Oglio, an Italian Jesuit peace activist, who refounded a Christian monastery in a multi-religious land as a place where Christians and Muslims might come together. Out in the desert, high on a hill, monks lead people in common prayer across uncommon texts—living, working, and worshiping together as witness to the boundless love God has for humanity. The monastery is not only a site for monks and those committed to living the life of prayer, but a house of hospitality for pilgrims of all faiths and convictions to encounter one another in the delicate spacing of intimacy and distance. Such a site, away from the world, fostering intimacy across lines of difference, was a healing presence for those who found themselves at Dier Mar Musa, one of the oldest Christian churches in the world. Father Paolo's witness to love across religious lines is the kind of Christian love we're called to enact in following Jesus as the one whose love knew no bounds. The monastery is a site of healing and intimacy for any who wish to come. Like Father Paolo, we might find ways of creating opportunities for interfaith and interracial intimacy in the places we find ourselves—in our schools, in our communities, in our nation.

But this world is weighted, as we know. And loving across lines of difference is not easy. And loving in the heart of a broken world, with all the weight that it might have, is even more difficult. Paolo Dall'Oglio's story continues. His monastery is situated in the desert of Syria. And back before we knew the name ISIS, when civil war first broke out, Father Paolo stood and defended those who had no voice. His love in the form of judgment against injustice required that he speak out publicly. That his proclamation was troubling to those with power is evidenced in his being exiled from Syria and returned to his homeland of Italy. But Father Paolo's heart was so broken by the conflict that he could not stay safely on Western soil; he returned to Syria in the hopes of being a presence of peace in an unsettled place. I cannot but think that Father Paolo saw himself enacting gospel forms of love in a weighted world, when intimacy compelled him to be a presence of healing and judgment but also love of enemy in the process of seeking peace.

Conflicting reports and uncertain communications have said that he has been killed; other accounts say that his kidnappers have kept him alive. We do not know his fate, but through the eyes of faith the Christian narrative allows us to see Paolo Dall'Oglio's life as a witness to the broken heart of Jesus poured out in love for a world in need. "This is my body, given up for you." This is the heart of the gospel message: the creative force at the heart of creation loves across all boundaries and faithfulness to this vision of love to the end is possible.

Paolo Dall'Oglio is a reminder of Jesus's love command as it moves from intimacy to distance, from a carefully cultivated love of the other to the places where love required love of enemy. Perhaps he was guided by the echoes of Jesus haunting him with the words "Love your enemies. . . . For if you love those who love you, what reward do you have?" (Matt 5:44, 46). Even further, Father Paolo's witness is a reminder of what everyday Christians might be doing in their liturgical spaces and in their lives, cultivating the practices of love of enemy: "Love your enemies, do good to those who hate you, bless those who curse you, pray for those who abuse you. . . . If you love those who love you, what credit is that to you? For even sinners love those who love them" (Luke 6:27, 32). Christian liturgical practices might lead to practical action in the world guided by the exhortation to "love your enemies, do good, and lend, expecting nothing in return" (Luke 6:35).

The multi-form of gospel love that we have been tracing illuminates the way that love is embodied and embedded. It is no mere feeling but rather a transformative power to be actualized in the world. Love, fostered in intimacy, mobilized toward healing, incorporating judgment out into love of enemy necessarily moves from the interpersonal to the structural and into the political. Mark Taylor's "agonistic political" invites us to see the relationship among these spheres, as an ontologically interconnected reality is the network within which we are situated. We struggle for recognition, for our well-being, too often at the eclipse of others. The struggle for well-being on the personal level is political as we seek to secure resources for our personal security under interconnected conditions in which resources must be shared. Gospel love as interpersonal inversely also calls us to a love of enemy that is necessarily political. In a world where we have created value-laden oppositions such that *enemy* by definition is outside the horizon of our care, the Christian call to love without boundaries will be a political move.

The powerful possibility of love of enemy is not merely a practice of disinterested self-giving; love of enemy bespeaks a practice that aims at deescalating the powerful pull toward the piling on of weight. Love of enemy invites a practice that might call forth not retribution but a different pattern of love in the world. A distinctive episode in Luke links love and forgiveness in the story of the woman identified as a sinner who anointed Jesus's feet and was blessed with forgiveness and admiration. "Therefore, I tell you, her sins, which were many, have been forgiven; hence she has shown great love. But the one to whom little is forgiven, loves little" (7:47). In response to our weighted world Christians are called to the great love that appears to be foolishness, for it is the great love of enemy, the prayer for those who persecute us. But the hope is that, like the one whose many sins are forgiven, the trespassing enemy, once forgiven, will be able to show great love in return. That is the God-healing love that Jesus demonstrates, and the God-healing love to which Christians are called.

For without the bold move of love of enemy, how are *our* sins to be forgiven? How could we ever be saved from the many sins *we* have enacted in shifting the weight of the world? Forgive us our trespasses, as we forgive those who trespass against us.

We arrive at a thread from the New Testament account that will be required in dismantling the value-laden oppositions that plague and yet structure our world, for all of the narrative of love throughout the Gospels is accompanied by the strain of forgiveness. King reflected on this essential component of Christian love for a weighted world. If we are not to set loose the cycle of escalation in retribution, Christian love requires both active love in repairing the world and active forgiveness for the harms that have been done. King invites us to contemplate:

> Few words in the New Testament more clearly and solemnly express the magnanimity of Jesus's spirit than that sublime utterance from the cross, "Father, forgive them; for they know not what they do." This is love at its best.
>
> We shall not fully understand the great meaning of Jesus's prayer unless we first notice that the text opens with the word "then." The verse immediately preceding reads thus: "And when they were come to the place, which is called Calvary, there they crucified him, and the malefactors, one on the right hand and the other on the left." Then said Jesus, "Father, forgive them." *Then*—when he was being plunged into the abyss of nagging agony. *Then*—when man had stooped to his worst. *Then*—when he was dying, a most ignominious death. *Then*—when the wicked hands of the creature had dared to crucify the only begotten Son of the Creator. Then said Jesus, "Father, forgive them." That "then" might well have been otherwise. He could have said, "Father, get even with them," or "Father, let loose the mighty thunderbolts of righteous wrath and destroy them," or "Father, open the flood gates of justice and permit the staggering avalanche of retribution to pour upon them." But

none of these was his response. Though subjected to inexpressible agony, suffering excruciating pain, and despised and rejected, nevertheless, he cried, "Father, forgive them."[22]

While King reminds us of the powerful witness of the Crucified One, he also maintains that love is not neutral and it does not hold back judgment. For if it were, love would turn itself over to a weighted world. But, love of enemy is different from indifference. Love of enemy does not relinquish judgment, but in judgment maintains love. The witness of Paolo Dall'Oglio attests to this. He was outspoken against practices and policies that crucified people, but he nevertheless pursued a path of peacemaking in that volatile situation. The witness of Mamie Till similarly insists that love of enemy does not relinquish judgment, but neither does judgment require hatred of enemy.

I return to Till's story because her witness is not just that of a mother grieving for her crucified son, whose haunting witness transformed our world. Mamie Till is an example of what it looks like to have the courage to love in a weighted world in all the manifold expressions to which the Christian gospel witnesses. An ordinary woman transformed to extraordinary love, she pursued the path of intimacy, judgment, healing, and love of enemy.

The intimate joy Mamie Till shared in the life of her son, Emmett, was a joy that expanded through both close and extended family, with neighbors and with friends. Her memoir makes it abundantly clear that loving Emmett was a project into which a whole network of people were drawn: an intergenerational, interracial network of people whose lives were enhanced by their encounters with this young boy. Not extraordinary people, but ordinary lives of the relatives who shared in his care; the neighbors who participated in his fun; the iceman and the milkman

---

[22] Martin Luther King, Jr., "Love in Action," in *Strength to Love*, 31–32.

who gave him nickels for his efforts to help them. Intimate love is not an isolated project but a vast network of lives that give life to our own.

If the work of love is not isolated, Mamie Till discovered also that the work of judgment and justice is not isolated either. At the painfully dark moment of confronting the race hatred in the Mississippi town that was home to her son's murderers, Mamie Till met the many, many workers for justice who contributed their piece to the project. Through her we meet the wealthy and generous Dr. T. R. M. Howard whose estate provided educational and recreational opportunities for the local Black community and whose work provided training for local nurses "so they could take advantage of the greater job opportunities they might find in the big city."[23] Dr. Howard was a leader in local civil rights organizing, and through him we meet political figures like Congressman William Dawson of Chicago, Congressman Charles Diggs of Detroit, and NAACP Counsel Thurgood Marshall. The organizing work introduces us also to Medgar Evers, NAACP field secretary; Ruby Hurley, NAACP's Southeastern regional secretary; and more NAACP people like Amzie Moore and Aaron Henry, whose names we may never have encountered but whose work on the ground transformed our White Christian nation toward greater racial justice. In Mamie Till's words,

> These people were heroic, but never seemed to have time to stop and think about how special they were. They just did what they did, it seemed, because they couldn't help doing it. I would come to understand and appreciate them and their bravery as I learned just what was being put on the line down there in Mississippi, and how it all related to Emmett and to me.[24]

---

[23] In Mamie Till-Mobley and Christopher Benson, *Death of Innocence: The Story of the Hate Crime that Changed America* (New York: Random House 2003), 152.

[24] Ibid., 154.

In the lynching death and trial we come to know the countless people who courageously played their part in working for justice. Black journalists denied seats in the courtroom, but courageously defying judge's orders and capturing the trial on film. African American eyewitnesses—Add Reed, Amanda Bradley, and Willie Reed—who were willing to testify against White perpetrators and the White establishment, even though it would mean giving up everything and relocating away from their homes.

> He was the first of the surprise witnesses called by the state that Thursday. And Willie Reed looked so nervous about it. He should have been. There was a lot at stake for him. There was a lot at stake for the trial. A whole lot. Of all the witnesses who would testify that day, he was the one who held the link that would connect all the other stories. And, with all the threats and intimidation that had surrounded this whole event, it was going to take a special kind of courage for Willie to take the stand. To tell the story. He looked nervous, but somewhere deep down inside him, Willie Reed had that courage.[25]

What kind of courage does it take to enact the love of judgment, knowing that one's life will be under threat and livelihood compromised, in order to see that justice be done? In the impossible balance of love of enemy and justice we learn the courage that is necessary to pursue Jesus's care for the least to its fulfillment.

Despite the defendants admission of kidnapping fourteen-year-old Emmett Till, and despite the coroners report that the disfigured body dragged from the Tallahatchie River with a barbed-wire noose and gin fan around his neck was Emmett Till's, and despite Mamie Till's intimate examination of her beloved son's body in its disfigured state—his tongue bloated from river water, an eyeball missing, his skull cut open from ear to ear—and her

---

[25] Ibid., 182.

positively identifying him, the jury returned a not guilty verdict. She recalls:

> The jurors deliberated one hour and seven minutes. They took a soda pop break, it was said, to stretch it out a little, make it look better. They reached their verdict. Not guilty. . . . In the end, the jury said, they did not think the state had proved that the body was Emmett's.[26]

I can think of few moments that rival this one in its affront to intimacy, the thwarting of healing, and the refusal of judgment made possible by ideologies, structures, and systems of White supremacy.

Yet, despite the injustice that was rendered in her son's murder trial, Till dedicated herself as a teacher in the cause of racial justice. She was willing to transmute her mother-love into a form of other-love that was committed to teaching young people to learn from history and to be emboldened in the courage to love toward the transformation of racism's long darkness. What kind of courage did it take for her to transform anger into redemption, desolation into resurrection? Mamie Till enacted the path of love in a weighted world. As an ordinary woman in extraordinary circumstances, she stands as witness to the power and possibility of love to transform our world: love that is intimate, and healing, with judgment and love of enemy. As her witness demonstrates, love in a weighted world takes courage, but it also takes everyday practices. And in Mamie Till's witness, we learn that love in a weighted world is possible.[27]

---

[26] Ibid., 189.

[27] Mamie's Till's love in world weighted by race hatred was more recently evidenced in the courageous expression of Nadine Collier, whose mother was among those killed by a White supremacist in Charleston, South Carolina, on June 17, 2015. Collier's words to her mother's murderer: "I forgive you. You took something very precious away from me. I will never get to talk to her ever again—but I forgive

HOW TO LOVE IN A WEIGHTED WORLD

Our world is weighted. Ontologically, at the very basis of our being, reality possesses a weight that might be enacted as bodies in balance, as networks of relationship and material well-being that enable both intimacy and distance. This weight might be shared equally among us as limited, finite human beings experience the joy and the struggle of our being in the world. Our existence is not a given; we all struggle in the face of our finitude. We will all get sick, we will all age, we will all die. In the time allotted to us we all need material sustenance from the world around us—we are dependent upon the light and the air and the trees and the earth to produce materials that will clothe, house, and feed us. We all rely on one another to experience the recognition that it takes to make us human. We all—every one of us finite human beings—struggle to find our way in the world, both materially and emotionally.

In the light of our ontological constitution as finite, weighted humanity necessarily struggling for our survival, we are also intimately linked to earth and the other so that we cannot make our way through this life without drawing on that which is outside the self. We are intimately linked to earth and the other, and we struggle for our survival within this linked reality. As human beings we are capable of sharing the weight of the struggle—being in balance with one another and with the earth. The fundamental way of balance that Jesus of Nazareth calls upon Christians to follow is the way of love—love of God, self, and neighbor that honors the intimate linkages and all the component parts.

---

you, and have mercy on your soul. . . . You hurt me. You hurt a lot of people. If God forgives you, I forgive you" (Elahe Izadi, "The Powerful Words of Forgiveness Delivered to Dylann Roof by Victims' Relatives," *Washington Post* [June 19, 2015]). Both Till and Collier were nurtured in the intimacy of Christian communities fostering love in its many forms and mobilizing this love toward the deescalating forgiveness of love of enemy in the context of race hatred.

Christians from the first century to the twenty-first century have been called forth to love within the confines of a weighted world.

But Christians in the modern era have radically failed in their epic task to love. White Christians mobilized Christian identity to see themselves as the pinnacle of God's sliding scale of creation. They mobilized Christian identity to give themselves priority over their Black and Brown neighbors. They put forth a Christian love that denigrated, rather than lifted, their Asian and Arab sisters and brothers. This inversion of Christ's practice in the practices of Christians mobilized the theological to transform the political so that the weight of the world was lifted from the shoulders of White American Christians, and others were crammed, crowded, extinguished, and exiled.

As theological and political, the reversal of this mockery of love must also be theological and political. We must rethink our theology and redo our policy. As the lives of everyday Christians can show, this is possible. The options for Christian love in a weighted world range from minimal participation in voting for legislation that will undo the damage that has been done to the maximum of martyrdom. Everywhere in between there are countless ways contemporary Christians might love in a weighted world.

Despite the reality of racial injustice and religious intolerance that shapes our world, nevertheless, I hope for a world that facilitates an inbreaking of the kingdom of God. A world that moves eschatologically toward "racial reconciliation [as] a divine gift and promise, partially realized here on earth and of certain fulfillment in a time known only to God."[28] This would be a world where bodily integrity, health, recreation, education, and economic opportunity are equally accessible to all, a world in which we could truly love our neighbor as ourself.

So, how are we to live? While this exploration has followed the path of Jesus to invite Christians to love in a weighted world, this invitation is necessarily against the backdrop of mystery. Our

---

[28] Bryan Massingale, *Racial Justice and the Catholic Church* (Maryknoll, NY: Orbis Books, 2010), 128.

universe is too vast, our history too complex, and our humanity too opaque for us to know with certainty the right way to live. Nevertheless, out of this mystery humans engage with the fundamental creativity of the universe in the process of meaning making that aligns them with what they have experienced. We exist. We may not have asked to be here, but we are here.

I meditate, therefore, on the question of my contingency and the possibilities for my self-creativity. I am here. Each day is a grace in the awesome mystery that my lungs can fill with oxygen and my heart beats. Although I can affect these fundamental sustaining realities from the outside with what I eat and how I exercise, it is not I who created the conditions for my breathing and my beating heart. All the while, there is something pulsing that sustains me. In the Hindu tradition, Anantanand Rambachan tells us, this pulsing of breath is the closest we can image the reality of God.[29] In the tradition of Islam, God is nearer to me than my jugular vein (Qur'an, Surah 50:17)—a power coursing through me, sustaining the universe and all that exists within it. In Christian poetics, God is the pulsating beat of the universe taking up residence in my own beating heart. All that is, is love; all there is, is love. In face of the mystery that is our existence, we might rest in the gratuitousness of it all—the sheer gift that there is something and not nothing—and we might respond with gratitude at the grace.

> Heaven and earth are linked together as truly as body and soul. We begin to live again each morning, we rise from the dead, the sun rises, spring comes around, and then resurrection. And the great study of how truly to become the children of God, to be made like God, to participate in the life of God, this is the study of the retreat. It is a painful study.[30]

---

[29] Anantanand Rambachan, "To Recognize and Love God in All: An Introduction to Hinduism," in *Five Voices, Five Faiths: An Interfaith Primer*, ed. Amanda Millay Hughes (Cambridge, MA: Crowley Publications, 2005), 15–16.

[30] Day, *On Pilgrimage*, 220.

It is a difficult study, in the midst of our struggles as human beings, to come to an affirmation of the goodness of our lives and the awesome source of a grace-filled world. Christians come to an awareness of a grace-filled world and name its awesome source God. The practices of human living are to honor that Source by participating in and taking joy in life, and emanating gratitude in our living. "We must practice the presence of God," Dorothy Day once wrote.[31] Practicing the presence of God as love is not easy, but it is the call of Christians where love is an intimate, as well as a public healing presence, where love requires both judgment and love of enemy. Christians may call themselves people of faith, but they ought to be called to be people of love.

What would it look like for us to bond together, as people of love, across the boundaries of race and religion, to see ourselves intimately intertwined with *all* people of love? To hear the stories of love as they are passed on through Buddhist tradition and through Hindu wisdom? To listen attentively to the stories of our Jewish and Muslim sisters and brothers as they enact love in the world? To encounter the love of humanity of humanism, and the love of divinity in the range of religious traditions of the world? The person of Jesus offers wisdom for seekers after meaning: what it means to be human is to love. Learning to love, together with our neighbors of other faiths, we might follow the Christian call to love and so to transform our weighted world. In the darkness of days in a White Christian nation we hope that a new day might be on the horizon. For that new day, let us learn to love together.

---

[31] Day, *Selected Works*, 92.

INDEX

Acosta, José de, 7
Adams, John Quincy, 52–53
African Americans. *See* Blacks
agonistic political struggle, 96, 177
Alexander VI, Pope, 6–7
American Indians. *See* indigenous peoples
anti-Semitism, 105
Apostles' Creed, 137
Asians
  association with Whites seen as beneficial, 19
  Chinese immigrants, 1, 55–60, 143
  citizenship denied to, 79, 141
  exclusion of, 2, 60–61, 76
  Hoyt classification list, excluded from, 68
  post-1965 immigration policy, favoring, 62
  in religio-racial project of Kant, 15
Barndt, Joseph, 46, 78, 165–66
Barrows, John Henry, 25
Barth, Karl, 134
Beecher, Henry Ward, 150
Belford, John, 68
Benedict XVI, Pope. *See* Ratzinger, Joseph
Benton, Thomas Hart, 18–19, 20
Bernard of Clairvaux, Saint, 139, 143
Blacks
  Christianity and
    Black Christ imagery, 37

Black Christianity regarded as derivative, 63
  Catholic prejudice against Blacks, 64, 65, 68–70
  nobility, achieving through Christian efforts, 27
citizenship status of free Blacks, 55
curse of Ham justifying African enslavement, 10–11
dehumanization of, 99
as dispossessed, 64, 65
Hoyt classification list, low ranking on, 67
incarceration of, 81, 93
racial disparities
  economic disadvantages, 84, 85, 106
  education access, 90–91
  government sources denied to, 80
  homeownership opportunities as limited, 79, 86–87, 98
in Reconstruction Era, 141
in religio-racial project of Kant, 15, 16
See also slavery
Blum, Edward, 37, 150
Bonaventure, Saint, 139
Bouchard, James, 57
Brown, Michael Joseph, 112–13
Brownson, Orestes, 23
Buddhism, 36, 160
Burgos, Giovanni, 62
Burich, Keith, 48–49